AVA

A LIFE STORY

by
Charles Higham

DELACORTE PRESS / NEW YORK

Designed by Ann Spinelli

Library of Congress Cataloging in Publication Data

Higham, Charles
Ava: a life story.

"Ava Gardner films": p.
1. Gardner, Ava, 1922–   I. Title.
PN2287.G37H5   791.43'028'0924 [B]   74-8106

ISBN: 0-440-01394-1

Prologue

A LATE SUMMER EVENING, 1950. A low-slung Cadillac draws up to the Screenwriters' Club in London's West End, and a woman gets out. Her face is dead white, and her eyes are filled with shadows. She is wearing a simple black dress, flat shoes, no makeup, no jewelry. She walks into the club's downstairs bar, sits in a corner, and orders a vodka. Her dark brown hair, loose and ungroomed, tumbles over her face. Now and again she brushes back her hair, glances indifferently across to the bar where Anouk Aimée, the French star, is having a drink with the director Ronald Neame. It isn't certain if she recognizes them or not. She drinks on, looking bored and depressed.

A genial, well-built man in his fifties stops by her table. He is easily recognized: Nunnally Johnson, wit and Hollywood writer, author of the screenplay of John Steinbeck's *The Grapes of Wrath*. She glances up at something he says, and laughs. They go to the restaurant upstairs. There, they continue talking happily, but when she stops laughing—a loud, ecstatic roar, with head thrown back—shadows flood into the face. She gives an order to the waiter: steak. It is at a premium in heavily rationed postwar England, and she grimaces at the size. "Bring two more!" she shouts, and Johnson looks at her in astonishment before she begins laughing again.

Two-thirty in the morning, early February 1959. The Corinthian Room, a down-at-heel nightclub in Sydney, Australia. The heat is stifling, the rudimentary air conditioning system doesn't work, and on the pavement outside under the stare of neon, cockroaches swarm like a living carpet. At a table against a wall, the woman is talking to an elegantly dressed male companion, her press agent, David Hanna. Suddenly a reporter in a crumpled suit, camera slung over one shoulder, comes to the table, asks for an interview and a picture. She looks up suspiciously from beneath heavy, late-night eyelids. She curses, picks up her champagne glass, and throws it at the man so violently it shatters against his chest.

Summer 1972. A preview party announcing a season of director George Cukor's films at the Los Angeles County Museum. Looking more composed, more serene than 13 years earlier, the woman is clinging to the arm of Roddy McDowall, laughing at what must have been a very raunchy joke. She stops laughing, and this time the shadows that once filled the face have gone. The eyes are alive with light.

Three glimpses of Ava Gardner. Enough to provoke the desire to find out about her, to write a book about her. Her chief fascination is that she has always seemed to live her life right out there on the screen before our eyes. Her string of famous husbands and lovers, her drinking, her confessed self-destructive streak, her constant search for a man who can give her complete fulfillment as a woman have been echoed in her playing of such roles as Pandora in *Pandora and the Flying Dutchman, The Barefoot Contessa*, Lady Brett in Hemingway's *The Sun Also Rises*, Cynthia in Hemingway's *The Snows of Kilimanjaro*, the hotel-keeper Maxine Falk in *Night of the Iguana*. Her broad, earthy humor, her constantly shifting moods of gaiety and depression, her harshness and kindness, her suspiciousness and openness have all been laid out for us in her playing. She is an actress without a mask. She is a beauty who has exposed her soul in her playing. She has surrendered her privacy: her courage deserves saluting for that.

I have been fascinated by Ava Gardner from childhood: I first saw her in *Whistle Stop* when I was a child in the correct Victorian city of Cheltenham, England; when she walked across the screen, she seemed to epitomize the impossible, remote glamor of Hollywood. Unlike Lana Turner—or Hedy Lamarr, who had a coarseness not concealed by a mask of allure—Ava showed a remarkable poise and elegance. Though as a voracious reader of fan magazines I knew even then that she came from a Tobacco Road environment in the Deep South, I noticed that she had the style, the walk, the flair of a natural aristocrat. Years later, George Cukor was to say to me: "She's a real movie queen. When she walks across a sound stage she creates a sense of excitement, she *stirs the pulses*. It's as though she were 'born to the cloth,' she has that feeling of command, that control, that mark her down as an authentic star. Ava's a *gent*." In the rain and gloom of an English provincial town, writing movie reviews for a school magazine, I felt those same sentiments.

Writing this book, then, was an act of discovery, of seeking out the essence of a legendary American figure. I found that almost everyone I spoke to about her responded with the greatest warmth, kindness, and enthusiasm. Nobody disagreed with her own statement that she was only an average actress. Nobody slurred over her heavy drinking, her remarkable list of lovers, or her frequent use of bad language. But they all liked her, genuinely and not defensively, very much indeed. And the reason is that she is a woman who has lived without pretense, who has lived without lies, who has hated phonies desperately.

The problem for me as a writer was to sort out fact from fiction, to discover, so far as was possible, the truth behind the legend. I had, in common with everyone else, been hearing gossip for years about her supposed nymphomania, lesbianism, alcoholism, her unreliability, her neurotic behavior on and off the set. I determined that secondary information, from newspapers and magazines, should be clearly labeled as such, and that I would draw my information chiefly from those who knew her.

I determined also not to "straighten out" the manifold contradictions in her nature: the mixture of masochism and passion for good living, the melancholia and the bursts of humor, the contempt for picture-making and the need to "make good" with every part she played, the search for aloneness and the hunger for constant company, the gypsy-like traveling and the endless reiteration that what she wanted more than anything else was to settle down with one man. And then the terror of having children, and the expressed need for a family.... Like that other *monstre sacré*, Orson Welles, she is deeply perverse, self-destructive, and her own worst enemy, as well as a loyal friend, an adorable companion, and the sweetest and most generous person in the world.

Writing this book, then, was a journey of discovery through a maze of contradictions. Long before I started these pages, I had talked to people about Ava Gardner. In Australia, in 1962, Mickey Rooney told me about his marriage. George Cukor discussed her as far back as 1961, Walter Chiari in 1967 and James Mason in 1968. Tony Perkins, on a visit to Hollywood to make a television film in 1970, talked to me about her in his trailer. Vincent Price (who called her the "Eternal Woman") has discussed her with me, on and off, for years. Kirk Douglas spoke of her at his house in Beverly Hills in 1971, the Burtons at the Directors' Guild preview of *The Sandpiper* 10 years ago.

I received almost no refusals for interviews. Susan Hayward was too seriously ill to be approached; Rossano Brazzi and Frank Sinatra ignored my letters; and Artie Shaw angrily rejected the simplest questions about his marriage to Ava. A few close friends in Hollywood, Spain, and London asked that their names not be used. Everyone else, either before or after the book was planned, spoke with impressive openness and explicitness about the star, seeking neither a removal of their names from the quotations nor an inspection of those quotations before publication. This freedom of utterance was remarkable in a book concerning a living person, and made the task of writing the biography much easier and more pleasurable.

Francisco Aranda in Spain, John Baxter in London, Giulio Cesare Castello in Rome, Colin Baskerville in Australia, Robert Mundy in Switzerland, Arthur Bell in New York, Elizabeth Antébi in Paris, and Peter Lev in Hollywood, all helped enormously. In North Carolina, Tom Lassiter, editor of the *Smithfield Herald*, was particularly helpful. I am especially grateful to Ava's Hollywood friend and mentor, the distinguished director John

Huston, for helping me to illuminate mysteries of character; to Nunnally Johnson—writer and wit—for a mine of information; to her directors—Léonide Moguy, John Brahm, the late William A. Seiter, Joseph L. Mankiewicz, the late Albert Lewin, the late Robert Siodmak, Henry King, Henry Koster, Stanley Kramer, Nicholas Ray, John Frankenheimer, Mervyn LeRoy, Robert Stevenson, the late John Ford, George Sidney; to producers Pandro S. Berman, Voldemar Vetluguin, Philip Yordan, Arthur Hornblow, Jr., Ray Stark; to cameramen Robert Surtees, Russell Metty, Joseph Ruttenberg, Jack Cardiff, Leon Shamroy, Freddie Young, the late Norbert Brodine, Giuseppe Rotunno; to press agents Milton Weiss, Les Peterson, Jim Merrick, Ann Straus, Emily Torshia; to Howard Strickling and Sidney Guilaroff (the latter saying almost nothing, but contriving thereby to say everything); to Ann Sothern, Edmond O'Brien (especially valuable on *The Killers*), Tom Drake, Deborah Kerr's diaries, Tony Franciosa (at a party for Rita Hayworth), Shelley Winters, Barbara Stanwyck, Dick Haymes, Howard Keel, Kathryn Grayson, Roddy McDowall, Charlton Heston, Fred Sidewater, Earl Wilson, Ruth Waterbury, Leatrice Fountain, George Eells, Phyllis Jackson, Joe Hyams (who with extraordinary generosity gave me access to his unpublished interviews with Ava Gardner), Silas Seadler, Howard Duff (remarkably frank on his long affair with the star), Robert Graves, Donald Richie (a marvelous Tokyo anecdote), Casey Robinson, and Gunnard Nelson.

David Hanna's published accounts of his tours with the star were of great value for continuity purposes. Ann Bloch heroically typed the complex manuscript and was helpful with numerous editing suggestions. Jeanne Bernkopf masterfully edited the manuscript as a whole.

Chapter 1

THE LITTLE TOWN OF Smithfield, North Carolina, stands midway between and below the communities of Raleigh-Durham and Wilson in the heart of the bright leaf country, so called because bright leaf, flue-cured tobacco, is grown here. It is a country of low, rolling green hills, grass-filled railroad tracks, red soil, and small, often derelict farms. Today, Smithfield's long main street is flanked by tawdry shops, hamburger joints, and self-important municipal buildings. The house lights still go out early at night, and by 11 p.m. the streets are deserted except for a few itinerants at the Greyhound Bus Station, a tramp or two, and a handful of people with nothing better to do than hang around the

late-night bars. Smithfield is the kind of town, just like a
thousand others, which, if you are a city person, you pass
through in a hurry on your way to somewhere else. There
is nothing remarkable about it at all, except for one thing:
it is the town where Ava Gardner was born on Christmas
Eve, 1922.

Or not exactly in Smithfield itself. She was born in a
satellite community so tiny it is not even visible on a
detailed local map: the settlement of Brogden. In 1922
Brogden was a sprawling patchwork of tenant farms, a
depressingly featureless place. She was the last of seven
children of a tall, bony farmer named Jonas Bailey Gardner, who could have stood as a model for Grant Wood:
with his lean, narrow face, long, skinny body, hairy,
stringy forearms extending from rolled-up gingham
sleeves, blue-gray overalls, and heavy workman's boots,
he was a classic picture of a Southern farmer. He had
green eyes and black hair, and a heavy dimple in his chin,
which Ava inherited. He was bigoted, particularly against
blacks, a devout Irish Catholic, and the fourth in a line of
tenant farmers. His life was a monotonous austere devotion to toil, devoid of any comfort except for his family.
His wife Mary Elizabeth (often called Molly) was, until
illness later made her thin and gaunt, a plumpish woman,
with brown hair and cold, haunted dark eyes; a puritanical hater of sex, she was born of a stern line of Scottish
Baptists, and there was iron in her pinched soul. She lived
in terror of most men but loved her husband and watched
him with fierce possessiveness.

Books were no part of the texture of their life: only the
Bible stood on the shelves, and it was not until Ava was
16 that she was permitted to read any novel not assigned
in school. She was a small, rather unattractive child with
carroty hair and a round, pouting face, not as striking as
the rest of her clan. Her eldest sister Beatrice (or Bappie,

as she was familiarly known) was a sturdy, healthy girl
with strong limbs; a decent, kindly person, she became second mother to Ava. Next came the jolly Elsie Mae; then
Inez; Raymond—killed when he accidentally tripped the
trigger of his father's rifle at the age of two; Melvin
(known familiarly as Jack), who later entered the State
Legislature of North Carolina; and Myra. Ava's earliest
memory was of the age of six, when Myra accidentally
hit her under the right eye with a hoe; the accident in-
stilled a lifelong terror of facial injury, which was to
emerge dramatically almost 30 years later in Spain.

The house in which Ava was born was a pleasant two
storey, four bedroom clapboard structure with a shingled
roof and eaves. The building was raised from the rough,
sandy ground on small piles of bricks. Frilly curtains and
pull-down blinds shaded the windows, which were tall
and narrow. Clumps of sagebrush grew in the rough
garden.

The rooms were high and airy, and the furnishings well
stuffed and comfortable in olives, greens, and grays, the
hardboard floors carpeted. Three hundred acres of farm
surrounded the house. The property included a sawmill
and a cotton gin, which Jonas Gardner operated until
early in the 1930s when a fire destroyed them both.

The countryside Ava first saw was a rolling patchwork
of brown and green, with cool hills far away, steam trains
puffing along the Atlantic Coast Railroad headed for Virginia, mules kicking up the soil, groves of pine and
patches of marshland. Those were still the lazy days when
old men lounged on benches and told their own or their
brothers' tales of the Civil War; when flies buzzed and
wasps burrowed into crab apples; when families came
home with baskets full of berries, their hands black as
though covered in dried blood. The sky she saw was often
alive with crows, and scarecrows, with their angular cruci-

fied arms hanging against the sky, were a common sight. The dominant colors of her world were yellow and red: the yellow of the bright leaf tobacco her father grew, the deep red of the soil.

Above all, her first memories were of the tobacco fields around the white frame house, and of the backbreaking work of most of the family to maintain them. She learned the names of the flue-cured tobacco raised in Brogden: Little Oronoco, Big Oronoco, Warne, Gooch, Adcock, Yellow Pryor, and Flanagan. She learned about the preparation and care of the seed beds, the rows laid three and one half or four feet apart, the plants set every two or three feet. She learned about the transplanting in May, the use of fertilizers—dried blood, ammonia, acid phosphate, sulfate of potash—and the ways of checking to see whether the tobacco was ripe at harvesting: the leaf surface had to show patches of yellow, the distinctive yellow of "bright leaf."

She must have been aware of poverty from the beginning. Though Jonas and Molly managed well enough, and Molly was a wonderful cook, there was always the awareness of the many tenant farmers who were struggling. There were the black settlements with shabby cabins, casually whitewashed. There were the settlements of poor white trash, down by the sluggish brown rivers or near the swamp country, with cottonmouth snakes wriggling through the blades of grass, or under the shadow of the live oaks, with their twisted limbs curling under cloaks of gray moss.

When Ava was growing up in the 1920s, tobacco was booming. By 1925, there were 283,482 tenant farmers in North Carolina, and so it became known as "the state of small farms." Tobacco had replaced cotton as the state's most valuable crop one year before Ava was born. Three hundred million pounds of leaf, or two fifths of the na-

tion's crop, were grown there in 1927. It was said that the
North Carolina crop was "worth more than all the wheat
in Kansas, or all the pigs in Iowa, or all the cotton in
Mississippi." But despite the boom, conditions were not
good. Soil—worked almost every day of a year—rapidly
became exhausted. There was a great waste of human,
horse, and machine power by primitive farming methods.

The Gardners were among the few stable families in an
atmosphere of bitter, restless migration. Yearly, in December, January, and February, tenants would pour into
North Carolina from Georgia and South Carolina, dot-
ting the roads with their swarms, while other families,
depressed by the fact that it was a buyers' market, moved
away. An observer in Smithfield in 1926 wrote: "This
wandering mass of humanity has no abiding interest in
any community because the tenants have no stake in the
land. They are strangers, sojourners, pilgrims, forever on
the move, and always discontented."

But for the Gardners, there were Sunday morning services at the small Baptist church in Brogden, Christmases
with the whole family gathered round, and long winter
evenings with Jonas Gardner telling stories. In the Twenties, the radio was a solace, and in 1932 Ava started
going to movies more often: she never forgot slipping
away secretly to see Clark Gable, Mary Astor, and Jean
Harlow in *Red Dust* at the local theater—the movie that
20 years later she would help remake with Gable himself.

It was an intensely happy family life until the Depression, when tobacco prices in the bright leaf country
plunged to nothing. Jonas sold the farm for a miserably
low price, and he and his wife began to quarrel bitterly.
Molly suddenly decided to leave her husband and take
Ava, aged 10, and her sister Myra. Molly took a job as
matron at a local "teacherage"—a boarding house for
teachers. Ava used to hang around the teacherage, bare-

foot, wearing cheap denims, her hair standing on end; often she would play pranks and stand on her head to astonish passersby.

Those who knew Ava at the time agree that she had no interest in book-learning, cooking or helping her mother with the housekeeping. She was much more interested in being a tomboy, running around in a harum-scarum fashion, or—a favorite occupation—climbing the Brogden rain tower. She used to play havoc with the various teachers who lived at the home. When she got older and went to Brogden Elementary School, she become known as a major tease of two middle-aged teachers, Mrs. Johnson and Mrs. Godwin. But it was all in good fun, and they adored her anyway. A great favorite of hers was Tommy Capp, who ran the Brogden general store. He used to sit next to the big potbellied iron stove and dandle her on his knee. Ava had been born four hours ahead of his son Raymond, and he regarded her practically as his own daughter.

In 1934, Molly moved to Newport News, Virginia, to run a boarding house for two years. Ava went to the Newport News High School and later to Smithfield High School, but she was not a very enthusiastic student, and proved so hopeless in plays she was fired from the casts.

Her first date was a handsome fellow student in the fifth grade, Luther Daugherty. She and Luther slipped each other brief notes in class—mostly "I Love You's" with hearts pierced with arrows. Unfortunately, she could not, unlike the other children, enjoy Luther's attentions in the "necking recess" at lunchtime; her mother insisted on her coming home to a hot lunch.

When Ava was 16, her father caught a mysterious virus and died; he was 61. After his death, Molly became moody, sullen, and withdrawn. She bitterly opposed Ava's seeing boys. She refused to buy her daughter new dresses or makeup: Ava wore the same coat for years. When Ava came home with a boy one night and let him embrace her passionately on the porch, Molly flung the door open, ordered the boy away, and poured so foul a stream of invective at Ava that she burst into tears. The experience had a traumatic effect on her, as had her father's death; it took her years to recover from these shocks.

At 16, despite what she said later ("Nobody ever wanted to take me out, no man ever looked at me"), she was a beautiful, leggy brunette in constant demand for dates. But under her mother's cold grip she seldom went out. And when she did, she clung to her virginity.

Those who knew the family say that the tension was constant and depressing, with Ava resenting being treated as a baby. She adored her mother but wanted to escape. She thought about becoming a nurse but decided she would suffer with the patients; she next planned to become a secretary. While her mother was matron at the teacherage in Rock Ridge near Wilson, she went to the Atlantic Christian College at Wilson, a co-educational institution. She took a course in business education and secretarial science and lived in the girls' dormitory. She took Gregg shorthand, office secretarial practice, advanced typewriting, and the composition of letters, and was considered shy and withdrawn by other pupils.

She attained the excellent shorthand speed of 120 words a minute. But some of the pupils made fun of her accent, more extreme than practically anybody else's there, and she was terrified of dating boys because of what the "consequences" might be. She became bored by the endless routine of the college, and the idea of becoming a secretary no longer appealed to her.

Her oldest sister Bappie had moved to New York and married a photographer, Larry Tarr. Bappie was at this time in her late twenties, with all of the strength, sureness, and authority that Ava lacked. "Bappie can do anything I can do, ten times better," Ava later told a close friend. "She was the real star in our family." Bappie was then, as she remains, Ava's staunchest friend and most loyal supporter, the one consistent touch of stability in Ava's stormy career.

At 17, Ava was a subdued, suspicious, and nervous girl: her mother's baby. She was simple, uneasy, raw. She had little poise, so self-conscious that she would have been a disaster at a sophisticated party. She had grown up too fast, and she was terrified of her own sexual attraction.

It was from her mother that she learned the lack of commitment to sexual existence that infuriated many men who loved her. An odd, disconcerting chastity lay at the very heart of her seemingly passionate character. Her mother taught her that she must love a man with such absolute devotion that he would not want to look elsewhere—yet taught her also to fear sex.

Ava was at 17 the victim of very American feelings: puritan romantic yearning, and a deep dread of poverty, the ultimate shame. Her conflicting emotions set the tone of her entire career: on one hand a desire for the romantic excitement of stardom, bred early by her furtive reading of fan magazines, and on the other a puritanical disgust at the cheap sentiment and sexual squalor of the screen, the sordid flesh-market of Hollywood; later, a scorning of the power and success that stardom so easily brought, and yet a horror of the possibility of being penniless, a horror that led her to take parts she despised.

In the early summer of 1941, when she was 18, Ava traveled to New York to visit Bappie and her husband at their apartment in the West 40s near Broadway. Bappie had made the apartment as comfortable as she could, and her Southern-style cooking was as wonderful as ever. But Ava was nervous in New York, worried because her mother was home ill, painfully conscious of her mother's concern that some man might take advantage of her. She stayed shyly under Larry's and Bappie's wing.

Needing a free model for photographs to use in window displays in the shop where he worked at 607 Fifth Avenue, Larry—a small, bouncing, energetic man with a broad Brooklyn accent—took shots of Ava. His pictures disclosed her to the most casual eye as a stunning beauty. She had not outgrown her awkward, clumsy adolescence, but her looks were startling. She had high, firm breasts and prominent nipples, a slender waist, and long, athletic limbs. She had green eyes, and her beautiful chestnut hair had a reddish glow. Her skin was intensely pale, like white jade, and she had perfectly even white teeth. Moreover, she had an enticingly slow, sulky smile and long, graceful hands. Her only awkward features were her poorly shaped feet; she liked to kick her shoes off since she could never find a pair which made her feel comfortable.

Columnist Ruth Waterbury, a friend of Ava's, said later: "Ava was not aware that Larry Tarr had put her picture in the window. She was furious. It was typically perverse of her that she should resent what many people would have been flattered by." The picture attracted a lot of attention from passersby. One of those was a stocky young errand clerk called Barney Duhan. Duhan said later: "I was working in the legal department of Metro-Goldwyn-Mayer at the time. I was running late for a party, and thought what lousy luck it was with my looks and my income that I didn't have a date for the party. I saw the picture—and said, out loud, 'Gee, wouldn't *she* be a fantastic date! Maybe I can get her telephone number!' So I went to a telephone on the corner and called the shop where the picture was.

"A woman, Mrs. Tarr, answered. I gulped and said, 'I'd like to meet that girl whose picture is in the window.' 'And who are you?' the lady snapped. I knew if I said I was an errand clerk she wouldn't have helped. So I lied in my teeth. I said, 'I'm a talent scout from M-G-M.' 'Oh, well that's different,' Mrs. Tarr said. 'But she just went back to North Carolina. If you want to see her I'll have her come up right away.' I panicked. If I sent for Ava now, how would I explain I was just an obscure errand clerk? So I said, smooth as you please, 'It's just a routine inquiry. But send me the pictures and I'll show them to Marvin Schenck, who's in charge of talent.' "

Duhan did show the picture to Schenck. He was impressed, and so was Howard Dietz, the powerful publicity chief. They asked Tarr and Duhan if Ava would be agreeable to a screen test. Ava took the train back to New York. She accompanied Bappie to an interview with Schenck at the New York office of Metro, and underwent the ordeal of a test.

M-G-M representative Ben Jacobson gave her a script to read. Pete Martin of the *Saturday Evening Post* witnessed the audition. He said later: "When she started reading nobody in that whole office could understand a word she was saying. She not only had the South in her mouth but a large slice of North Carolina's farming country as well! When Jacobson asked her name, she replied, 'Aa-vuh-Gahdn-uh.' She dropped her g's like magnolia blossoms."

Martin reported Jacobson's saying to Ava: "We'll make a silent test of you. If I send a sound track out to the Coast with nothing on it but vocal spoonbread, they'll have my head examined."

Jacobson and Marvin Schenck gave instructions that

Ava should have the best lighting available—the kind of glamorous lighting used for such M-G-M stars as Greer Garson and Hedy Lamarr. Al Altman, experienced test director, handled the job of making Ava look fairly presentable. He said later: "She couldn't pick up a glass, cross her legs, or even say her own name with any conviction. She was lousy. I told her, 'Look up, Ava, look down, smile.' She couldn't do anything. I put a vase on a table. I told her to pick up some flowers. I told her to sit down in a chair and emote. We all looked at each other and shook our heads. She was hopeless."

M-G-M publicist Silas Seadler adds: "Maybe she looked hopeless when Al shot it. But when we ran the test—you never saw anything like it. She just took our collective breaths away. There wasn't a man there wouldn't have liked to take her to bed. Clumsy she may have been, talk she could not, and thank God the test was silent. But what a dame! We sent the print off to Hollywood telling them all they were nutty if they didn't sign her. And meanwhile, she went home to mother!"

Chapter 2

S EVERAL MEMBERS OF the M-G-M publicity staff remember what happened after the test was approved by Marvin Schenck. Ben Jacobson said later: "Ava said, 'Ok, so I got through the test. So I may be going to Hollywood now. Well, if I make it there, I'll tell you what I'll do. I'll marry the biggest movie star in the world!'

"One of our staff went into an adjoining office and came back with a photograph behind his back. 'Would you like to see the greatest star in the world?' he asked. 'Sure,' she replied as she perched on the edge of a desk. I think she was under the impression she was going to see a picture of Clark Gable. She'd had a childhood crush on him.

"Then Bill whipped out the picture. She nearly died. It was a full-length picture of Mickey Rooney!"

Three days later the print of the silent test arrived in Hollywood. George Sidney, later a famous producer-director, had the job of selecting new starlets for the studio. He ran the test. He says today: "She was terrible, as everyone says. Ordinarily I guess we'd have patted her on the head and told her to apply to the stenographic pool. But there was something about her. That girl had a style, a way of moving, that seemed to come across. And of course her sex appeal was stunning.

"I can remember going to one of my assistants and saying, 'Tell New York to ship her out! She's a good piece of merchandise!' "

A few days later, Ava started out on the train for California with Bappie and a young press agent, Milton Weiss. "Her mother would not let her go unless her elder sister went along with her," Weiss says. "So Bappie Tarr came as chaperone. Not that it was necessary. Ava was as cool as an icicle about men. I wouldn't have stood a chance with her."

He adds: "Ava was at once terrified and excited at the idea of making the trip. I think she really wanted to go to Hollywood and make good. Like every young girl, she was turned on by the idea of meeting big movie stars. But at the same time she knew she had no acting experience, nothing behind her at all. I guess she felt if she didn't make it she could always get a job as a secretary back home. I think it was just the idea of going 'Hollywood' that kept her on that train at all!"

The shock came when Ava arrived and found that "Hollywood" was just a dreary, sleepy suburb of Los Angeles, with shabby palm trees, pale, washed-out buildings, tacky dime stores, and garish theaters, a far cry from the razzle-dazzle of New York or even the rural beauty of North Carolina. She was further shocked by the Hollywood Wilcox, a cheap hotel which at her promised salary of $75 a week was all she could afford. The furniture in her small room looking down over Selma Avenue—a depressing thoroughfare which later became the haunt of dope addicts and male prostitutes—consisted of badly varnished plywood, and the carpet had a stain on it. It was certainly no better than any small hotel in Smithfield.

Even Metro-Goldwyn-Mayer was scarcely more impressive. Situated in the suburb Culver City, surrounded by ugly buildings which dated from the first years of the century, it was a jumble of semiclassical structures, barn-like sound stages, and tiny, twisting streets filled with men on bicycles. The very first thing she saw as she drove in with Milton Weiss was a mortuary just inside the gates. "That's a good beginning," she said wryly to Milton.

Once inside the studio's sprawling, biscuit-colored Irving Thalberg Building, Ava was rushed into another test: this time with sound. George Sidney directed it, and Ava walked clumsily through it, more or less repeating the standard gestures she had made in her silent test. She talked a little about her background in her Tarheel accent, and Sidney could barely understand a word she said. He ran the test for Louis B. Mayer. "She can't act, she can't talk, she's terrific," was Mayer's response to the extraordinary sexual magnetism she exuded. "Give her to Gertrude [Gertrude Vogeler, the voice coach] and Lillian [Lillian Burns, the dramatic coach] and let her have a year's training. Then test her again," Mayer said, as he rose to leave the screening.

That evening Milton Weiss tried to ease the shock of the newcomer's arrival by taking Ava to a party at the home of Ruth Waterbury, the famous columnist of the *New York Daily News*. Ruth's small and unpretentious home was situated on Woodrow Wilson Drive in the

Hollywood Hills, with a sweeping view of unspoiled canyons and an attractive rose garden. Ava walked into a room filled with prosperous, middle-aged Hollywood businessmen and their wives. She stood, looking remarkably ill-at-ease, holding a drink. Then a strange thing happened. "Each of the men in the room began circling around her like tomcats in heat, leaving their wives looking at each other," Ruth Waterbury remembers. "Within an hour, the wives had insisted on taking their husbands home. Ava, Milton Weiss, and I were alone."

Next day, Weiss drove Ava to the studio. Several productions were being shot that July of 1941: among them, *Babes in Arms*, with Mickey Rooney, *When Ladies Meet*, with Joan Crawford and Greer Garson, and *H. M. Pulham Esquire*, with Robert Young and Hedy Lamarr.

Every sound stage was buzzing with activity, and at lunchtime the commissary swarmed with stars. The studio was run from the giant office of Louis B. Mayer, the squat, ugly, hard-bitten studio boss who cried sentimentally over Andy Hardy pictures but would fire a recalcitrant executive at the drop of a balance sheet. He was the subject of many Hollywood stories: when Joan Crawford walked in his office one day she said, "Don't you normally stand when a lady enters the room?" and the tiny man replied, "Madam, I *am* standing"; and told by another star that there were "too many Jews overrunning the studio," he snapped back, "What do you think I am, a Hibernian?"

When Ava was ushered into Mayer's enormous office, Mayer gave her a lecture on moral behavior that made her head spin. But he saw to it that she was signed to a seven year contract by the legal department: at $75 a week,* with options every six months. Every time her option was taken up she would be advanced according to

* Some sources say $50.

her presumed box-office potential. She had to agree to all roles she was given, all promotion called for by the studio, and any travel thought necessary for her star status. There was a morals clause which specified she must never become drunk, commit indecencies, or misbehave in any way in public. A publicity release was written about her, declaring her to be a Powers model, and her born name was given as "Lucy Johnson," so that people would think Ava Gardner was a publicity department invention.

Each morning, Ava clocked in with the other starlets at around 6:30, and went into makeup under the supervision of the chief of the department, Jack Dawn. She accepted his ministrations with a lazy, sardonic detachment, sometimes joking with him about the masks he made of her face, sometimes yawning openly during the long sessions as her eyebrows were narrowed down, her eyelashes carefully enhanced, her cheeks given the illusion of very high cheekbones, her heavily dimpled chin de-emphasized by careful application of powder. Dawn used blue, green, or brown mascara stroked on in three coats, each coat given time to dry thoroughly. A hair wave-set was used to turn up her eyelashes. Her hair, loose and windblown, was brushed and lacquered by the chief expert in the field, Sidney Guilaroff, who later became a great friend of Ava's.

It was Louis B. Mayer's wish that every new starlet be made to feel part of the "M-G-M family," and that any rough edges be honed down at once. The result, unfortunately, tended to eliminate the personality of a new player, at least on the screen. M-G-M women looked so well groomed and ironed they were virtually store window dummies. By the time Jack Dawn had removed all of the flaws in her face and Sidney Guilaroff had made her hair look as smooth as a race horse's mane, Ava Gardner was as standardized as the rest.

Her screen appearances were entirely confined to walk-ons while the grooming went on. Before long she was attempting to purr in a regulation Hollywood siren's voice: low, subtle, subdued. She was learning to talk "for the screen," in a voice no higher than she would use if she were talking to someone half a foot from her nose. But to the end of her career, her voice remained her weakest feature.

The greatest figure in the star-training scheme, the person who worked with actors and actresses like Tom Drake, Van Johnson, Donna Reed, Kathryn Grayson, and Lana Turner, was the remarkable Lillian Burns. Trained in the grand theatrical tradition by Lillian Bayliss, *doyenne* of Shakespearean teachers in England, Miss Burns was solely responsible for teaching the young players at the studio. Small, fiery, rather like Bette Davis in appearance, dynamic in her attack on the problems of performance, she was the most powerful single force in Ava Gardner's life at the time.

Lillian Burns did not follow the pattern of other studios of seating young actors and actresses in front of a teacher in class and training them as a group. She believed in each player's being taught individually. The only exception to her rule was that each Friday she held a day-long class for all of the major contract players. They would select among themselves a well-known scene they wished to play, and act it out for her. At the end, she would make both severe criticisms and constructive suggestions, and the entire scene would be redone until it was perfect. It was played in her huge office, while she watched herself teaching in a mirror beside her desk. When Louis B. Mayer suggested that she should use a proscenium arch in class, she swept the idea aside: she wanted to reproduce the conditions of a sound stage, as close as possible to that with which the actors would be faced when they were actually under the gaze of the cameras.

As she did with the other players, Lillian Burns took Ava aside for an hour or 90 minutes each day and gave her detailed instructions. Ava's natural magnetism and beauty were her only assets. She had literally to be created as an actress from the ground up. Lillian Burns had to teach her how to move so that every movement attracted attention. She had to discover what natural gifts Ava had—she laughed attractively, she had a charming animal quality, she would tuck one leg under her as she sat on a chair, a habit she unconsciously copied from Lillian Burns—and make these work for the screen so that they appealed to audiences. Just as she trained Lana Turner to use her slightly subdued and breathy voice and her "little girl" eagerness to make the sinful things she did on screen seem touching and forgivable, she had to train Ava to understand her sexuality, her lazy feline grace, and punch these home without self-consciousness or self-mockery. David Belasco had long ago given Lillian Burns the precept on which she worked with Ava. When Lillian, aged 14, had asked him, "Does acting come from the pit of the stomach?" he had said, "No. Further down." It was Lillian Burns' ultimate technique to make Ava realize that her acting must come not only from her mind, her eyes, her stomach; it must be felt from her sexual center. She needed this quality of sexual tension and invitation.

Aside from her hours in the hair and makeup departments and her hours with her voice coach and her dramatic coach, Ava had to work with the publicist Ann Straus in the photographic department, posing for photographs by such experts as Clarence Bull, Eric Carpenter, and Edward Hurrell in the drab studios set aside for stills in the administration building.

Ann Straus remembers: "Sometimes after standing with her leg up for hours in cheesecake shots Ava would turn and cling tight to my arm and ask, 'Do I have to do this?' 'You know you do,' I would answer. 'But can't I be an actress? Do I have to be a clotheshorse?' 'Wait and you'll get a chance. Get out of the studio now and there'll be nothing.'" Ava listened, and they became very close friends.

The portrait cameramen asked her to make her eyes into slits and poke out her lower lip to give an impression of sultry sexiness. They had her wet her lower lip slightly with the tip of her tongue. "I have to work on this high-powered art," she said. Ann Straus says, "Ava told me often that the whole business of being groomed for stardom was absurd and perhaps just a touch disgusting."

Ava also posed outside the studio in bathing suits. She told *Photoplay Magazine*: "You could have carpeted Hollywood Boulevard with my pictures from curb to curb. I don't remember how many swimsuits I wore out —without getting near the water. I shot enough sultry looks around the M-G-M photo gallery to melt the North Pole." Her attitude to her work was always laconic. After she stood for a shot at the pool of the Beverly-Wilshire Hotel, she heard a woman guest saying, "Disgusting! How can she pose in those shameless two-piece bathing suits?" "So you don't like two pieces?" Ava snapped. "Which one would you like me to remove?"

On top of all her other work, Ava took a grueling series of dance lessons. She studied classical ballet and modern dance with enthusiasm. She assumed the classic stance—breasts jutting forward, head erect and chin high, back pencil-straight—which came to mark her as a star. Her body became a supremely disciplined instrument of M-G-M's collective will.

Ava's attitude to all this work was defensive, sometimes harsh and unhelpful. "But she really wanted to succeed," Ann Straus says. "Her indifference was a pose. Her drive was extraordinary and ruthless. She was determined to put up with all the nonsense to become a star."

She submitted to everything except Metro's rigid dietary requirements. While every other girl on the payroll obediently ate a monotonous diet of cottage cheese and fruit, she dug into a massive series of meals including her favorite—fried chicken, hominy grits, hot biscuits—at 6 a.m. At lunch, she was again ravenously hungry and would have Louis B. Mayer soup (obligatory for all players, as it was a recipe of his mother's), mixed green salad, two glasses of milk—she hated it, but felt it was good for her—and a large slice of apple pie. At the afternoon tea break at four, while Norma Shearer or Greer Garson took one cup without milk or sugar, she shocked everyone by indulging in a massive banana split, until wartime restrictions made that impossible. She loved vegetables, especially collards and black-eyed peas cooked in their shells. One source of her amazing vitality was an old custom, learned in Smithfield, of drinking the juice of cooked vegetables or soaking it up in slices of corn bread, Southern style and home-baked. She also liked fresh fruit salads, raisins, and nuts. She refused the studio's demand that she do calisthenics but instead plunged into outdoor sports, playing tennis, golf, and badminton every weekend and when she was not required for scenes.

Chapter 3

I T WAS DURING THIS basic training that Ava met Mickey Rooney.

Milton Weiss recalls: "I'll never forget how she first met Mickey. We went over to the *Babes on Broadway* set where Mickey was working. It was her first week at the studio, and she was getting the regulation tour we gave all the starlets.

"We saw this fantastic guy rolling his eyes in drag, dressed up as Carmen Miranda with a fruit hat bigger than himself, a bolero, a slit skirt, and enormous platform-soled shoes. It was Mickey! Well, drag or no drag, Mickey was the studio's number one lady killer, and when he took one look at Ava, he was horny as hell. He had to have her!"

That day at lunch, Mickey was sitting in the commissary with his entourage, including his stand-in, Dick Paxton, Andy McIntire, Sid Miller, his publicity men, Alan Gordon and Les Peterson. Mickey was dazzled by Ava, but the others told him it was quite obvious from the way she looked at him she wasn't attracted to him. But he wasn't to be put down: she had given him a hint of some interest, with a casual flicker of a cool glance. What if every man at the studio would have given a month's salary to spend a night with her? Wasn't he the biggest star in the world?

He had always suffered from an acute, indeed an agonizing, inferiority complex. Brilliantly gifted, beginning as a child star as Joe Yule, Jr., he had been part of the M-G-M factory for more than six years. He had risen to fame in the Andy Hardy series: the innocuous tales about a small-town boy which were the favorites of Louis B. Mayer. He was a dynamo: he sang, danced, acted comedy or tragedy with astonishing versatility and an energy which hid his deep inner bitterness and sense of depression at his lack of physical stature and intellect.

He was terrified of being alone, needed the constant flattery and support of his "circle." He dreaded interviews, and yet the moment a reporter arrived, he "proved" himself as a man of intelligence by talking loudly and rapidly on every subject under the sun, stumping about on his tiny legs, his back held straight, his head high, his manner overpowering. His onslaught on Ava was like that of a baby chimpanzee on a giraffe. Though she was a penniless unknown and he was the immensely rich king of the lot, she appeared to look down on him from a height he could not possibly reach.

Ava's attitude to Mickey was extremely complex. Ruth Waterbury says: "Her motives in wanting to date Mickey were very mixed. On the one hand, she wanted to keep her joking bet made in New York that she would marry the biggest box-office star in Hollywood. There was probably a good deal of ambition mixed up in her motives. After all, for an obscure starlet to make it with the biggest star would have been a tremendous coup for her. But it would be completely wrong to say that she used Mickey, or that she twisted him around her little finger for success. In fact, she was genuinely taken with his charm."

Ava's technique of studied indifference suggests that she had made up her mind to marry him from the outset. Whereas many other starlets at M-G-M would willingly have gone to bed with him to further a career, Ava must have known that by not doing just that, she would ensure his total commitment to her. There was nothing hard, calculating, or cynical in her campaign. She was genuinely pleased with him. She really thought it would be fun to marry him.

Years later, I asked Mickey about his relationship with Ava. In 1962 he was at a low ebb in his career, on a nightclub tour of Australia with the dancer Bobby Van. With a potbelly, a balding head, and a rasping voice, he had little left of the young Andy Hardy except the superb performing talent and a ferocious, now rather desperate energy. He still talked, as he had then, like a machine gun, throwing out ideas, some inept, others inspired, about everything from Washington politics to an Australian picture in which he planned to co-star with a boxing kangaroo. "I pressed Ava with notes, gifts, phone calls, but she remained as aloof as ever. Finally, at what I guess she found an embarrassing request, accompanied by some mugging and comedy, from me, she smilingly said she 'might' let me date her.

"I was beside myself. I told my gang I would marry her if it killed me!"

After several days of futile pressure, Ava gave in and asked Mickey to have dinner with her and Bappie at an apartment they had just moved into on Franklin Avenue. Next night, the three went to Chasen's. Ava and Bappie were greatly amused by Mickey's wit, imitations, and Hollywood stories. Years later, Ava told the journalist Joe Hyams: "His kind of courtship was as foreign to me as the caviar at Romanoff's, the spaghetti at Ralph's, or the Zombies at Don the Beachcomber's. Like those Zombies, he had a powerful effect. He was the original laugh-a-minute boy and even the second or third time round his stories, jokes, and gags were funny. There wasn't a minute when he wasn't on stage.

"Occasionally a shrill voice would sound in my brain warning that maybe life with Mickey would be like life on a sound stage. That he'd always be 'on.' But whenever the warning sounded Mickey drowned it out with a new joke."

She received other warnings as well. Louis B. Mayer called her in as soon as he got word of the romance, and carpeted her: he was furious that his biggest star would marry an obscure contract girl. Ava stood trembling on the other side of his vast desk while he snarled at her, "Once he gets into your pants he'll be tired of you and he'll chase after some other broad." Then he turned her over to his scarcely less ferocious assistant, Ida Koverman, who said to her on her master's orders, "I hope you know what you're getting into if you marry Mickey."

But by December 1941, Ava was determined, come hell or high water, to marry Mickey. She was fascinated by him, and he was totally infatuated with her physically. Not realizing that she had already made up her mind, he kept up a rat-tat-tat campaign to pulverize her into submission for marriage. Day after day he continued to pick her up at home: many evenings he drove her to his home in Encino to visit his family. At nightclubs they did the rounds repeatedly while he sang, played drums, told jokes incessantly. He wore himself out wooing her, and she let him.

She told journalist Pete Martin: "At first, Mickey's shortness kind of stunned me. But he's a gentleman when he's courting a lady. The trouble is he's telling you how to do things all the time. If you ask him the hour of day, he's apt to build you a clock.

"Mickey was 'on' all the time and I tried to be a good audience."

He sent her bouquets of 100 roses at a time and sprays of orchids. His bills at restaurants, where he ordered champagne, caviar, and her favorite, crêpes suzette, often were as much as $150 a night, and the nightclub drink bills were equally astronomical. He proposed to her 25 times in as many dates, and each time she brushed him off with a "You're crazy."

Exactly at what moment she finally said "yes" has not been remembered by anyone. Almost certainly, it was after he dropped her off one night at her Franklin Avenue apartment, and once again pressed his suit. Shrugging, languid, she drawled an "Okay." He jumped in the air.

Louis B. Mayer was infuriated when he heard that Mickey had given Ava a diamond engagement ring, but in view of his favorite star's enormous public success he decided it would be unwise to unsettle him. Luckily, M-G-M had in release *Life Begins for Andy Hardy*, which was practically the Mickey Rooney story on the screen. *Babes on Broadway* was rushed to a conclusion so that Mickey could wed Ava. Mayer flung a massive stag party for him shortly after Pearl Harbor; there was jocular and unprint-able marital advice from such stars as Clark Gable, Walter Pidgeon, and Robert Taylor. Mickey said later that at the end of the colorful toasts to his manly prowess, he said, "Thanks, you horny bastards. The first guy I see looking hard at Mrs. Rooney gets a right hand to the teeth."

To handle the marriage arrangements, Louis B. Mayer appointed the young press agent Les Peterson who had worked with Mickey before. The complete "company man"—eating, drinking and sleeping Metro-Goldwyn-Mayer—Peterson had a very engaging directness, modesty, and the ability to calm the nerves of difficult stars.

Today, Peterson is almost completely blind and lives in a tiny apartment in a housing settlement for retired people in Laguna Hills, California. His charm, his humor, his sweetness of character remain intact, as he runs his fingers over pictures of Ava and Mickey, trying to "read" them, remembering things that happened over 30 years ago. He says: "Mayer instructed me to see to it that the marriage was arranged discreetly, as privately as possible, and well out of town. I was to find an apartment for Mickey and Ava in a suitable location, since residence at the Encino house would attract too much attention. I was even to pick out the wedding band, and to accompany the couple on their honeymoon to protect them against snoopers and reporters.

"After I'd found a platinum band which Mickey approved, I chose an apartment in a building on Wilshire Boulevard near Westwood—Wilshire-Palms—which was jointly owned by Red Skelton and the director Frank Borzage." The apartment had white walls, white carpets, large mirrors, beige leatherette chairs. It was a rather drab, subdued two-bedroom first-floor flat with little to recommend it. But it was the least likely target for the publicity hounds who scoured Bel Air and Beverly Hills, and it was within easy distance of the Westwood previews of Mickey's pictures.

After weeks of searching, Peterson also found an ideal

location for the wedding. It was a small white Presbyterian church in the town of Ballard, tucked away in the foothills of the Santa Ynez Mountains, a chain of green and blue peaks which towered over Santa Barbara on the Pacific Coast. Peterson drove into Santa Barbara early in January 1942, and swore the local newspapers to secrecy in return for the promise of exclusive pictures to be prepared by an M-G-M photographer.

The wedding took place on January 10, almost exactly six months from the day that Ava came to Hollywood. The wedding party left Los Angeles in two cars. The party included Mickey Rooney's father Joe Yule, Sr., his mother Nell Pankey, his stepfather, and Bappie. On the way in from Los Angeles, they stopped at Carpinteria, near Santa Barbara, where Mickey called Santa Barbara County Clerk J. E. Lewis to ask him to prepare a license. On special request, Lewis drove to his house on Channel Drive in Montecito, where he handed Mickey the papers. Then the party drove on to Ballard.

The wedding was performed by the Rev. Glenn H. Lutz, a chubby, beaming man who is now Presbyterian minister in Las Vegas. Mickey was so nervous during the ceremony he almost dropped the wedding ring on the floor while trying to slide it onto Ava's finger. Mrs. Lutz pounded away on the upright the Wedding March of Mendelssohn and "I Love You Truly." Ava wore a simple blue costume and a corsage of orchids; Mickey wore a dark gray suit with a polka dot tie, a white carnation in his buttonhole, and a white handkerchief peeking out of his top pocket.

Ava told Joe Hyams: "My only disappointment with the wedding was that I didn't have a white wedding dress to wear. I had dreamed of getting married at a beautiful ceremony dressed in a beautiful gown. I didn't mind missing out on the big wedding but I did miss the dress.

Unfortunately, I didn't have enough money of my own to buy a dress and I had no intention of asking Mickey for it."

Les Peterson says: "From the mountains of Carpinteria, Mickey drove Ava and me to the place I had chosen for the honeymoon: the Del Monte Hotel near Carmel, where Deanna Durbin and Vaughn Paul had also honeymooned. The others all returned to Los Angeles in the second car. That evening, after Mickey and Ava had checked in, I drove off in Mickey's car to see my family in San Jose, leaving the couple alone."

Once alone with Mickey in their suite, Ava was terrified. She felt all of her mother's horror of sex welling up in her. Mickey, despite his experience with women, was equally terrified. He put on his pajamas back to front, becoming entangled in the arms and legs. When he came into the room from the bathroom Ava was lying in a long white nightgown, covered from head to foot, like a figure on a tomb. Awkwardly, clumsily, as he confessed later, Mickey began to make love to her, and he gradually overcame her shyness. But it was only when he actually penetrated her that he learned the incredible truth: the beautiful woman he held in his arms was a virgin.

The next few days were painfully difficult for Ava. Despite the joy she showed in the photographs taken on the honeymoon, she was often despondent as Mickey ran off to the golf course and left her alone for long periods. Away from his Hollywood friends, he called them constantly by long distance. All Ava could do was provide "love talk." Les Peterson kept her company during Mickey's absences, but he was no substitute for a husband. Since she had no money with her, Les bought her ice cream or chocolate sodas.

At last the difficult, lonely honeymoon was over, and

the Rooneys and Les Peterson set out on a long and complicated M-G-M promotion tour for the Andy Hardy series.

Les Peterson remembers: "From Carmel we drove to San Francisco, where we read the shocking news of the death of Carole Lombard in an air crash on her way to Indianapolis on a bond tour. We stayed at the Palace Hotel and saw the local sights for two days. Then my wife arrived by train, picked up Mickey's car, and drove it back to Encino, while the rest of us proceeded by Santa Fe Super Chief to New York. In New York, we stayed at the New Yorker Hotel; Mickey and I were old friends of the proprietor, Carl Snyder, and we had a wonderful time with Snyder, his wife, and his daughter Suzie. At a press conference at the hotel, Ava sat in a deep chair while Mickey sat on the arm; that way, the difference in their heights was not too apparent. Ava and Bappie went shopping for new dresses for President Roosevelt's birthday celebrations in Washington.

"From New York, we proceeded to Boston, where Mickey entertained for the Red Feather Drive Community Chest, and then went on to North Carolina. Mickey and I stayed at Fort Bragg, where Mickey entertained the troops, while Ava went on to Smithfield to see her family.

"Then came the greatest excitement of the trip. Ava and Mickey had lunch at the White House with Roosevelt.

"After the President's birthday celebrations and Mickey's appearance for some war bond drives, he and Ava returned to the apartment I had picked out in Westwood."

Once they were settled in Westwood, Mickey and Ava were miserable. They had satisfied the physical side of the relationship, and each had proved the one could win the other: the conquest was over and there was little to take its place. Mickey wanted to go on living as he had before, dashing around in fast cars with his gang of friends, drinking, and gambling at the racetrack. Ava wanted to sit at home with him and listen to phonograph records. It was a hopeless situation.

Ava told Joe Hyams: "Mickey and I were children. We had no idea that marriage involved a meeting of minds. That it involved sharing of problems, planning together, making a life together."

Mickey told me: "I loved Ava. But I was too immature I guess to be married to anybody. I wanted to have the most beautiful girl in the world as my wife but I wasn't ready for her. I didn't understand her too well nor she me. I wanted to go out at night and have fun, as well as having the domestic benefits. I thought the world owed me the best living—a lovely girl at home and everything else as well. I woke up—fast!"

Ava said later: "I did everything humanly possible to make my marriage to Mickey work. He was 'on stage' all the time and I was careful not to offer him any competition. I was his greatest audience, at home or out. I cooked for him and I cleaned for him. I puffed up his ego at the expense of mine many times. I was a devoted, loyal, and good wife in every sense of the word.

"But, I was demanding. I didn't expect more than I wanted to give but I did expect that much in return. Also, I think I'm enough companionship for my husband. I didn't like being on the go every minute of the day with parties, clubs, and dinners nightly. But I'm not the kind of wife who likes to sit home alone nights, so on those occasions when Mickey wanted to 'be with the boys' I sat home—and burned.

"It's hard to tell simply what makes a marriage go wrong. My marriage to Mickey was sour before it began. I think I knew long before Mickey and I were married

The birthplace of Ava Gardner in Brogden, North Carolina; Ava's sisters, Mrs. John A. Grimes, of Smithfield *(left)*, and Mrs. D. L. Creech, of the Brogden community *(right)*, are in the yard, talking with the present occupant of the house
(PHOTO BY BERNADETTE HOYLE, SMITHFIELD, N.C.)

Family album photo
of Ava, age 12
(COURTESY, JOE HYAMS)

At age 13 (COURTESY, JOE HYAMS)

Opposite: Ava, 15, on the beach with her mother (COURTESY, JOE HYAMS)

Left: Ava at 16 (COURTESY, JOE HYAMS). *Opposite*: Three on a honeymoon. Mickey, Les Peterson, and Ava in Carmel, California, January 1942 (COURTESY, LES PETERSON). *Below*: Wedding picture. Bappie, Ava, Mickey, Rev. Glenn H. Lutz, Les Peterson (COURTESY, LES PETERSON)

that we weren't meant for each other. I was stupid enough to think marriage changes a man. I know better now."

In a desperate move to save the marriage, Mickey leased a cottage on Stone Canyon Road, Bel Air. He still drove to the studio each day, he to appear in *The Courtship of Andy Hardy*, full of exploitable parallels with his real life romance and marriage, and *A Yank at Eton*, she to appear in walk-ons as a hat check girl or model or to make more appearances in Ann Straus' cheesecake layouts.

Mickey told me: "When we returned at night, Ava wanted to kick off her shoes, tie up her hair, and relax in a casual sweater and skirt. She wanted to show her prowess in the kitchen, but I dreaded the long evenings in which she would sit silently writing letters home or chatting about home-town facts, or just sitting. Talking to her was like talking to a brick wall; she would agree with what I said, then sink into silence again."

Ava in her turn was aggravated by his talk about golf, the racetrack, the work at the studio. Understandably, he fled night after night, and equally understandably, she sulked over uneaten dinners or lay on her bed in an agony of the recurrent stomach pains she had had since childhood.

The brutal fact was they had almost nothing in common. Mickey wrote later how Ava would sit in corners at parties silent and sad while he dazzled the crowd. He also told how she dreaded having a baby (her version was that he was opposed to her having one). He described a horrible scene in his memoirs: after they returned from a party and went to bed, she jumped up suddenly and warned him, "If I ever get pregnant, I'll kill you."

It was clear that by this time she was so maddened by his selfishness that she could not have endured giving birth to his child. He recorded later that she even cut the furniture with a knife when he was out late one night.

Yet despite the grievous problems of their declining marriage, Mickey helped Ava enormously in her career. Ava said later: "I was green as grass about everything. Half my time on the set I was trying not to cry. Because I didn't know how to do what they wanted I'd get sulky." Years later, she told the famous columnist Adela Rogers St. Johns: "When I got my first walk-on in *We Were Dancing*, Mickey showed me how to walk, how to stand, what to do with my hands, how to ignore the camera. If I ever do anything big, I'll owe it to Mickey. Even though he didn't understand marriage, he sure as hell understood show business!"

As a result of Mickey's pressure, Ava began to get small parts. In *Two Girls and a Sailor* she was a canteen hostess who falls asleep as she dances. In *Reunion in France* she was a fashion model in a salon patronized by Joan Crawford.

Though her training was completed and she was married to the studio's biggest star, she was still regarded as a chattel. She very much resented the studio's ironing-out of her personality. Her remarks about it to friends were snappish and sometimes unprintable. But she wasn't foolish enough to let any of these remarks, even in a watered-down form, see publication; she relentlessly stuck to her working schedule, coolly biding her time until better parts should come along.

"People like Ava and myself were treated as properties," says the quiet and gentle actor Tom Drake, sitting in a cafe in Hollywood. "I remember one publicity man at the studio saying, 'They are the only merchandise that leaves the store at night.' We were *merchandise*.

"The pressures were constant at the studio. An assistant was always hovering at the gate to make sure we stars arrived on time, we were taken by the arm and rushed at once into makeup. There was an overwhelming atmosphere of terror. The actor was the one cog in the wheel upon whom everyone depended: if anything went wrong with the cog the entire operation fell apart. If visiting reporters came in and took up five minutes of a star's time, efficiency experts hovered around, looking at their watches and agonizing over the lost moments. Over everyone hung the terrifying image of the 'lost' star Luise Rainer, who had been fired and blacklisted by Mayer, after winning two Oscars in a row."

Drake adds: "Ava asked me, 'Why was Rainer dismissed?' Many people believed that it was because she had tampered with the 'cuts' of her films, changing scenes to improve her own image. Others said she had refused to make love to Louis B. Mayer. Nobody knew for certain.

"If Louis B. Mayer appeared on set everyone froze, turned into puppets. They looked as though if a string was pulled, their heads would turn sideways. It was horrible."

Shortly after a preview of Chaplin's recently revived *Modern Times* that February, Ava was stricken with agonizing pains in her stomach. At first, she thought they were once again the pains she had experienced from emotional causes since childhood. But the symptoms became so excruciating she had to be rushed to the Hollywood Hospital, where she was operated on for an inflamed appendix. Only a few days later, she was back at work.

It was obvious by the latter part of 1942 that the marriage would not last out its first year. Mickey's absences from home grew more and more frequent. Barely eight months after the wedding, it was all over.

Ava forcibly ejected him from the house in Bel Air,

then moved out of it herself—back to the apartment in Westwood which the studio still retained.

Mickey called her constantly, waking her at night, and she became terrified of his demands that he return to her. To protect herself against him, she asked a close friend from the studio, Leatrice Carney, daughter of the famous silent star John Gilbert, to move in with her.

"Our lives were very simple," Leatrice says. "We would get up very early in the morning and drive in our separate cars to the studio. Ava and I took turns to cook breakfast —just an egg each, that's all. In the evening, friends would drop over: the attorney Jerry Rosenthal, who would sometimes go into another room with Ava and I'd hear them discussing her affairs in murmurs, and his wife Ruth; Tony Owen, who married Donna Reed; Fran— Mrs. Van—Heflin; Minna Wallis. We'd cook dinner together, just steaks in a pan, nothing ambitious. We weren't in the least domestic.

"My chief memory of the time I was there, maybe five months, was Ava's terror of Mickey coming to 'get' her. One night her fears became a reality. He literally broke the door down when she wouldn't let him in. We had to struggle with him to get him to leave. I think he was crazy with frustration because she wouldn't sleep with him. He wanted her so badly, but she no longer would have anything to do with him."

After the collapse of a reconciliation attempt, Ava filed suit for divorce on May 2, 1943. The complaint, prepared by her attorney Alo G. Ritter, charged that Mickey caused Ava "grievous mental suffering" and was "guilty of extreme mental cruelty."

On May 21, 1943, Ava finally won her decree in Superior Judge Thurmond Clarke's court in downtown Los Angeles. Asked of what Mickey's "cruelty" consisted,

Ava said, "He wanted no home life with me. He told me so many times."

Also Ritter asked her in the witness box, "Is it true that he left you alone much of the time?"

She said tearfully, "Yes, he did. He often remained away from home. Twice he stayed away for long periods. He spent a month with his mother once and when I protested he told me he simply didn't want to be with me."

To everyone's surprise she suddenly waived all her previous claims to half of Mickey's property, insisting that what she wanted was $25,000, a car, the furs and jewelry he had already given her.

Bappie also testified to Mickey's long absences from home, and the case was closed. Ava was told it would be a year before the divorce was final.

Next morning, she received a telegram from home. Her mother, after a gallant fight against breast cancer, had died in agony on May 21, the day of the divorce hearing. Ava flew to the funeral and sobbed piteously as the simple coffin was lowered into the grave.

Chapter 4

DURING THE YEAR THAT followed the divorce, Ava stayed in the apartment in Westwood, working on a series of forgettable films at Metro, in which she appeared seductively gowned in party scenes. She was still only a step above the extra level. A brief loan-out to Monogram, the cheapest studio in Hollywood, to appear with the East Side Kids in *Ghosts on the Loose* was no help. Bappie moved in with her, after Leatrice Carney left, and waited patiently each evening until Ava came home after a day's shooting.

A stream of bachelors and unhappily married men dated Ava: among them, Jimmy McHugh, Lee McGregor, Turhan Bey, John Carroll, and Robert Walker.

She was photographed at Ciro's, Romanoff's and the Mocambo, where the Argentinian Fernando Lamas taught her to tango. Peter Lawford was a "frequent companion." Most of these dates meant absolutely nothing to her. But pictures of her with these idols of the time were valuable publicity, the men were handsome and spent freely, and she was determined to have a good time.

After the divorce, Ava began to have regrets. She and Mickey began to date again, and were seen in most of the nightspots. Interviewed by the *Los Angeles Examiner* at the Hollywood Palladium, where they shared a table, Rooney said, "I love Ava a great deal. Maybe we'll be reconciled. We're young yet, and both of us are glad that we caught our domestic error in time to correct it for a long and happy life together."

Ava clutched Mickey's hand and said, "That's right. I couldn't get along without Mickey. And I guess he couldn't get along without me."

Meanwhile, Ava was beginning to get speaking parts. At last she managed to get a real break: a role that called for more than just walking on, though it certainly did not call for major acting. She was assigned to *Three Men in White*, in the famous Dr. Gillespie series about a lovable old curmudgeon of a doctor played by Lionel Barrymore. It was directed by Willis Goldbeck, whose previous career as a writer had gone all the way back to the silents. Goldbeck gave Ava a great deal of sympathetic help in her role. She played the part of a girl who is used by Gillespie to vamp Van Johnson—an intern applicant for the job of Gillespie's assistant—in order to see if he will prove to have the strength of character to resist her. In one scene she pretends to be a lush, dragged into the hospital in the middle of the night. Soon, Johnson discovers she is in fact a sweet girl with an invalid mother she supports. Her performance was charming: under Lillian Burns' scrupulous guidance, she was convincingly beat-up and besotted as an alcoholic, and she played the scenes of seduction with a cool, poised sense of comedy, easily outacting Marilyn Maxwell, the other seductress engaged to test Van Johnson's resistance. The preview at the Village Theater in Westwood was an immediate sensation. Bobbysoxers crowded the theater; the boys gave loud wolf whistles whenever Ava came on the screen, and the girls did not seem jealous, only envious in a very friendly spirit.

The trade press threw hats in the air: the *Hollywood Reporter* said, "Marilyn Maxwell and Ava Gardner, two of the smoothest young sirens to be found . . . are superb, and should delight the studio with their histrionic conduct here," and *Variety* was equally enthusiastic.

As soon as *Three Men in White* was released, Ava was rushed into *Maisie Goes to Reno*, an entertaining trifle starring Ann Sothern as Maisie, in which Ava played the millionairess wife of Tom Drake. Ava walked through the part with a straight Lillian Burns back and a haughty manner.

Despite the fact that the public and the trade press loved her, Ava was treated harshly by the papers as a whole, and by Bosley Crowther of *The New York Times* in particular. He launched a campaign against her, repeating such words as "abominable," "weak," "sultry but stupid."

And despite the warmth of manner she brought to these parts, Ava was bored with them. They meant nothing to her; she was doing scenes in which she had not the slightest interest. The inane lines she had to speak—lines she had waited to speak for four years—aggravated her unbearably. She felt an intense self-hatred; she could well understand why Robert Young, who had acted in vapid roles for years, had become an alcoholic. The sterile streets, hard sunlight, and shabby palms of Los Angeles numbed her with boredom. But she drove to the studio each morning shortly after dawn, determined to go on until she achieved star status.

Tom Drake says: "Like everyone else at Metro, Ava felt ambiguous about the studio. On the one hand she hated its autocracy, on the other she appreciated the fact that it was the greatest star-making machine of all. Of course she always *said* she wanted to go back to North Carolina and be a secretary, find a good, dull man, and raise kids. But you *knew* she didn't mean it."

Her insomnia began, partly the result of her once deep sleep being interrupted by the roar of traffic past the windows of the apartment overlooking Wilshire Boulevard. She entertained infrequently; evenings when she was not dating she preferred to spend quietly with Bappie, listening to records, or at the pleasant home of Van and Frances Heflin. Sympathetic, subdued, Frances Heflin became, after Bappie, her closest confidante.

On June 14, 1944, Mickey and Ava dined together at the Palladium. The next morning, Mickey and 500 other United States Army recruits boarded a Pacific Electric train, Mickey comically hauling aboard a five-foot duffel bag almost the same size as himself. He was shipped off to Fort Riley, Texas, as a buck private; week after week he wrote letters to Ava begging her to restore the relationship. When she finally called him up and told him not to write anymore, he broke down in tears, so overcome with grief that all he could do was crawl onto his bunk and sob into the blankets. By his own confession, he was so tormented with the loss that he started to drink seriously for the first time in his life. But he could not blot out the pain.

While Mickey suffered in Texas, Ava discovered an extraordinary new lover: the multimillionaire aircraft and tool company magnate Howard Hughes.

In 1943, Hughes was a spindly, delicate six foot three inches and 158 pounds, terrified of physical injury or illness which could destroy his precarious constitution. He was so disturbed by the possible adverse effect that alcohol might have on him that he forbade anybody even to be seen drinking near him. His terror of germs was so pronounced that if anyone who had not just washed his hands attempted to touch him, he shrank away.

His right-hand man at the time, Noah Dietrich, today in his 80s and living in a fantastic Gothic castle perched above the Sunset Strip, surrounded by a barefoot maid, a healthily squalling grandchild and a plump gray cat, remembers Hughes at the time he met Ava: "He was the most boring man in the world. He had only two subjects of conversation: business and women's breasts. He had no interest in literature, art, music, or painting, or anything else in the field of culture. God knows he was not a gourmet. He ate exactly the same meals each day, scrambled eggs with milk for breakfast—no bacon or sausages —or occasionally some Post Toasties. No tea or coffee— he was afraid they contained poisons. For lunch he had sandwiches. For dinner he had one butterfly steak with tiny peas. He would take a small silver rake and go through the peas. If a pea didn't go through the prongs of the rake he rejected it immediately. Everything solid was cut into tiny pieces, because he feared that his delicate stomach wouldn't absorb it.

"You have to remember that for a man of his height, 158 pounds was far too little. He was painfully conscious of his sticklike, unmuscular arms, his equally sticklike legs, and his disproportionately large hands and feet. With $200 million he lived so frugally on that diet he might as well have been on relief.

"He had a very high sexual appetite, despite his frailty. But even there he was careful of his delicate frame. He would have his women—usually five or ten at one time, and some of them pretty famous—stashed in apartments or houses so he could visit them any time he wanted. He would arrive without much warning—the women were followed everywhere by bodyguards so they could be brought home at once if necessary—then he would get into bed with them, fuck them, and get out again, get dressed, and go home. He was afraid if he romped around too long he'd get tired and catch something. So no woman could ever call him a good cocksman.

"They liked him because they felt they could mother him. Ava was no exception. When he made it known he wanted her she gave in, not because of his money, but first and foremost because she liked thin dark men, and second because he awakened her motherly instinct. As for him, he was obsessed with big boobies, and she *had* big boobies. Of course, he was much too nervous and shy to make a date with her when he saw her in M-G-M B-pictures, which was why he got his henchman Johnny Myer to set up a meeting with her at a dinner party.

"He particularly wanted her because she'd just been married to Mickey. He had to have what we call 'a wet deck'—used goods."

How true this is, I, of course, have no way of knowing. Long since severed from Hughes' employ, Noah Dietrich's remarks are no doubt affected by the nature of his unhappy current relationship with Hughes. Ava took a more charitable view in an interview with Joe Hyams: "When Mickey and I broke up I was the loneliest girl in Hollywood. Then, I met Howard. A friend had been acting mysterious for days about the 'wonderful man' she wanted me to meet. At the time I wasn't interested in any man, wonderful or not, and I told her so.

"One day she caught me at the studio when I was feeling particularly down in the dumps and brought me to her home for dinner. A few other people showed up as if by magic, and my dinner partner, through no coincidence, turned out to be the 'wonderful man.' He was tall, average looking, plainly dressed, and nice in a humble way. I never did catch his name when we were introduced and all through the meal kept finding new ways to address him. We exchanged a few pleasantries and I thought him interesting but not exciting. He left abruptly at the dessert course.

"The next day my friend called and told me Howard was quite smitten with me. 'Howard who?' I asked. 'Howard Hughes, of course,' she said.

"I later learned the entire dinner party had been carefully arranged by Mr. Hughes so he and I could 'get to know each other.' I have since discovered that Mr. Hughes' ability to get things done for him is astonishing to say the least.

"Mr. Hughes was to reappear again and again in my life—usually when I needed him. An experienced man of the world, he can be a gentle and understanding friend. He makes it easy for you when you want ease; presses a button and there's a plane ready to take you anywhere in the world; another button and there's a hotel suite waiting for you. If you want to be quiet and left alone he arranges it. He's just the ticket for a girl like me—from the Deep South and lazy."

The lavish gifts, the sudden trips on private planes to Mexico, the visits to the Hughes mansion—later occupied by Ava's great friend, the writer Nunnally Johnson—in Beverly Hills: these were exciting for a still simple girl out of North Carolina.

But the relationship with Hughes was as stormy as the one with Mickey had been. "At first," a woman friend of Ava's, who will not give her name, says, "Howard was kindness itself to her. He would surprise her with telephone calls which he put through himself, from call boxes; I remember he was particularly fond of one set of call boxes in the Beverly Hills shopping center. He'd slip over there in a very modest car so as to be unobserved, pull his hat over his eyes, and slide inconspicuously into a box. With his mania for cleanliness, that was quite something: often the boxes were filthy.

"One time she requested a tub of orange ice cream— certainly a way of making him prove his love for her, as at that stage in the war even a President would have difficulty getting orange ice cream. Within two hours of the request an enormous limousine arrived at her front door and a uniformed chauffeur stepped out with a giant wastebasket-sized container of the best orange ice cream. Ava screamed!

"But then she began to lose her interest in Hughes sexually. It was a familiar pattern with her. In the first place, she wasn't in love with him at all, and if she wasn't in love, intense physical relationships with all of their demands were extremely difficult for her. Hughes was a strong, masculine, highly expert lover. But still she wasn't satisfied.

"Her essential remoteness, that 'hollow feeling' at the heart of the relationship, drove Hughes crazy, just as it did Mickey. They began to have the most terrible quarrels. He gave her a brand-new Cadillac, then took it back when she broke a date with him."

Noah Dietrich says: "He had her watched 24 hours a day by Mormon bodyguards, a night man and a day man. He always felt Mormons were more reliable than anybody else. For a while, she behaved. But soon she became restless. She imported a Mexican bullfighter to the house in Hollywood Hughes leased for her. One night after the bullfighter and her gang and his own friends had been dancing up a storm, he went drunkenly upstairs and

flopped on her bed. She fell asleep in the living room. She
came up to tell him she had some breakfast ready. He
was so angry with her for not being in bed with him when
he woke up he knocked her down the stairs. She fell to
the bottom and a friend of hers ran over to her, terrified
she might be seriously injured. She wasn't, but she lay
absolutely still and whispered, 'Don't try to move me. I
want him to think I'm dead.' The bullfighter was convinced she'd broken her neck and fled, never to come
back.

"Howard arrived in the midst of all this and told her to
get out of the house—he was disgusted by her behavior.
He screamed at her as she backed into the wall next to
her bedroom. He turned around to walk away. She said
something, and he turned around and slapped her so hard
she fell onto a sofa. She got up as he walked away again,
and grabbed the nearest thing at hand—a heavy orna-
mental vase. She struck him with it so hard she knocked
him out cold. His bodyguards carried him out to his car.
Next day, bag and baggage, she was unceremoniously
packed off to her apartment. Hughes was horrified not
only because she had entertained a man in her house but
because she was drunk—and he detested nothing more
than a drunken woman. But soon he was dating her
again.

"It's essential to realize that Hughes just thought of
Ava as a big pair of boobies and a good lay. That's why it
was very easy for him, even after she clunked him over
the head, to make up with her again. When he patched
things up he took her on trips to Mexico in his private
Boeing Stratoliner, with a bedroom at the back, a cocktail
bar, and easy chairs and sofas. Most of the time he'd be
up front piloting it himself, with Ava, dressed in a co-
pilot's costume and goggles, as a *very* excited companion.
Of course, one thing was rough on Ava: she mustn't

drink, these were 'dry' trips and the cocktail bar was stocked with Cokes!"

After the quarrel over the bullfighter, most of their evenings together were spent at Hughes' house. Years later, Ava returned there with Bappie and told Nunnally Johnson, her close friend who had acquired the house: "Christ! This brings on total recall. The arguments, the fights! But Howard could be the kindest and most generous man in the world."

By the beginning of 1945, the last year of the war, Ava was thoroughly depressed. The collapse of the marriage with Mickey Rooney, the tension of the affair with Howard Hughes, weighed her down. She tormented herself, friends say, over her own possessiveness in these relationships, her insecurity over her failure to be totally fulfilled in a relationship.

Gradually, in that period, her nature began to change. From being essentially a homebody, she began to be an addict of night life.

"Ava was the most constant and the most intense customer I ever had," says the ex-boss of Ciro's, Herman Hover. "She'd come in with a whole gang, or sometimes stag—she was one of the few Hollywood girls who'd dream of going stag—and she'd dance and talk to the bandleader and drink a few, and then she'd want to go on to a party afterward. She never misbehaved or got unseemly. Often I'd have her up to my big house in Beverly Hills with Lana Turner and other party-loving stars and we'd start all over again at three o'clock in the morning. No sex, just a lot of lewd jokes and laughter and fun. Then everyone would drag themselves off at dawn, Ava looking as good as new."

Part of the reason for this new way of life—Ava had always liked going out, but now she was going out nearly

every night Hughes did not date her—was to escape from
the oppressive weight of Hughes' interest in her. But it
was also brought on by her sharp sense of depression at
what M-G-M was doing to her. "After four years of crap,
and after I worked my ass off, what have they given me?"
she told a friend. "Second fiddle to Van Johnson, for
Christ's sake!"

But she had spoken too soon, too quickly discussing
her chances of ever being a serious actress.

Her chance arrived at the tail end of 1944, by very
circuitous means. Out of the blue, an opportunity came
which overnight turned her from being a mere Hollywood
starlet and girl-about-town into one of the legendary figures of the century. The opportunity was a tough Jewish
writer called Philip Yordan.

Today a millionaire wheeler-dealer in film properties,
for many years one of the highest paid Hollywood writer-
producers, in 1945 Yordan was a poverty-stricken be-
ginner. Desperate for a job, he was trying to set up a deal
whereby he would buy raw film stock with his savings
and sell it at a profit, and would include the right to make
a film on the stock itself. Since raw stock was at a premium at the end of the war, he believed he could swing a
deal. His agent, Charles Feldman, told him that Seymour
Nebenzal, a German producer at United Artists, was
looking for low-budget, offbeat films to make from prize-
winning plays or novels. "Just get something that won a
prize, and Sy'll jump at it and the raw stock," Feldman
said.

Yordan recalls today in his Beverly Hills Spanish
mansion: "The William Morris Agency had a novel
which had won the Avery Hopwood Award, *Whistle
Stop*. Nobody had read the damn thing and nobody
seemed to know who the hell Avery Hopwood was, but

Charlie Feldman found it could be bought very cheap—
for only $7500. With a decent name as the star, Feldman
thought some stock could be found and that a local bank,
the Security Pacific, would put up 60 percent of the budget at only 6 percent interest. Charlie had George Raft
under contract and added him to the package. Finally, I
actually *read* the novel. I was horrified. It dealt with a
young brother and sister who had sexual intercourse together and it was written in a high-flown, pretentious
style that made little sense. The male lead was an incestu-
ous young Adonis with blond hair. George Raft was over
40, had thinning hair and a potbelly. What the hell could
I do? I changed the story completely. Meanwhile, the
casting went on. It was crazy. Aside from his rotten
looks, Raft—with a New York accent—was supposed to
be playing a small-town guy in Wisconsin. And Victor
McLaglen was a bartender and was Scottish. And Tom
Conway, playing the guy who runs a local gambling joint,
was British. It was insane. Now we came to casting the
female lead.

"We couldn't find anybody suitable, which is a polite
way of saying no one wanted to play the part. Nebenzal
and I and our dates used to go to the Mocambo every
night. All of the 'in' movie crowd did. You could see
everyone there. And Ava was there all the time. Nebenzal
saw her there one night and said, 'She's doing nothing at
Metro, she looks great, why don't we use her?' I said,
'Fine.' I should argue? Five thousand to Metro, and the
dame was ours.

"Well, I talked to her, and I started to date her. She
was very nice, very generous, very kind. People with marital problems would just move into her apartment in
Westwood and take over. One night I came home with
her and the whole place was full of smoke. Some girl
had fallen asleep with a cigarette and set it on fire. Ava

didn't worry. She just saved the girl and helped put out the fire."

The affair with Yordan did not last. She had entered into it only to please him. Yordan was exasperated by Ava's lack of intellect, and she was bored by his shrewdness. She also sensed that he had no admiration for her talents, while he became annoyed by the fact that she had little interest in following his advice or attempts to educate her. "Ava was, quite simply, the most boring woman I have ever known," Yordan told me.

By the spring of 1945, Yordan had a finished script for *Whistle Stop*. He turned it into a persuasive and gripping story of a girl, Mary, with a mysterious and shady background who returns to a tiny whistle stop Illinois industrial town where her lover, played by George Raft, has become a loafer and a drunk. The owner of the local hotel and saloon becomes strongly attracted to Mary, while Mary's downbeaten lover is almost forced into theft and murder by a bartender. The ending shows Mary rescuing her friend from a life of crime.

The film's director was Léonide Moguy, whose method with actresses was infallible. With his profoundly French instinct for their vanities, egotisms, and electric charm, he drew them aside before the shooting and explained to them how they must allow their natural animalism to release itself without constraint or shame. He pointed out to Ava the sexlessness of so many American women: he had been struck by the fact that her M-G-M performances, constrained by the disciplines of Lillian Burns, had made her seem too much like a model with a book on her head. He wanted to teach her to revert to the unconscious animal grace she had before being put through the M-G-M mill. Luckily, she had enough native intelligence to see his point. Bit by bit, both before and during the action of the picture, he wore away her stilted manner. He saw to it that her rages, her insecurity, her sudden alarming changes of mood were brought out in her actual playing, that she showed the temperament, the glow, the presence of a star.

Whistle Stop's art director was a great veteran of the UFA studios in Berlin, Rudi Feld. The camerawork was by Russell Metty, a rough-and-ready, cigar-chewing man who later worked with Orson Welles. Both Metty and Moguy remember Ava with pleasure, saying in almost the same words that she was subdued, punctual, cooperative, professional.

But Philip Yordan feels differently: "Sure she was on time. But she didn't have the first idea of how to act. She was just a sweet, confused girl trying very hard not to be a hick, and failing.

"I'll never forget as long as I live—I still wake up with a nightmare about it—the first day on the picture. Nebenzal called me frantically and asked me to come to the set. When I arrived, it was horrible. Moguy was desperately trying to direct a sequence despite little or no command of English. I had written a scene in which Ava arrived from New York with a mink coat and a ring, and Raft was asking her who had given her these presents. Originally, it was a bitter, rather sophisticated sequence. But it was obvious that neither Raft nor Ava had the slightest idea how to speak the lines. I asked Moguy to call an early lunch break and I sat down and rewrote the entire scene in monosyllables. The dialogue then ran as follows: 'What's that?' 'A ring.' 'Where did you get it?' 'Chicago.' 'From whom?' 'A man.' 'What man?' etc. It was ghastly. Only by casting the lines in the most simple and primitive terms could Raft or Ava learn to speak them. Ava had absolutely no 'ear,' no idea of what she was saying," Yordan says. "Her voice was poor, thin, she was woefully miscast."

Ava was even more conscious of her shortcomings than Yordan was, calling Lillian Burns constantly at Metro, even driving long distances to consult with her at 7 a.m. before a day's work, lost, sick, and afraid in her new stardom. Her only support lay in the friendship of Moguy and his lovely Danish wife Daan. It was through Moguy that she really learned to respect a director for the first time.

When *Whistle Stop* was finished, Ava slipped into the Pomona preview disguised in a cheap scarf and sunglasses, and shuddered at her stiff and mannered acting. Yordan shuddered too. "I thought she was terrible," he says. But then Ava had an extraordinary experience. She noticed that the men around her—unaware of her presence there—were becoming visibly aroused by her beauty on the screen. She suddenly saw the sexual and commercial power she was capable of wielding. When she begged comment cards from the preview theater management— one probably apocryphal story had her writing "Excellent" on her own card—she was genuinely astonished. They read: "She's a knockout," "This new girl's dynamite," "Ava can come around any time," and "She's terrific."

The reviews were enthusiastic. *Variety* said: "Miss Gardner does her best work to date as the girl who must have her man." The *Motion Picture Herald* wrote: "With the dynamics of Gardner and Raft in it, *Whistle Stop* is certainly not a dull place." Other reviews were equally impressive.

Ava had to admit to herself that she was enormously pleased with the critics' response. At the very least, they would force M-G-M to realize she was more than a clotheshorse, that perhaps at last they would give her more chances to act.

Chapter 5

J UST BEFORE *Whistle Stop* was planned, Ava had met at the Mocambo Artie Shaw, a man who was to influence her deeply. At 34, Shaw was internationally famous as one of the most gifted bandleaders and clarinetists in America. His brilliant, stabbing style earned him rave reviews before he reached the age of 21. His 14-piece band was among the leading swing groups in the late 1930s and early 1940s. His records were best-sellers. Then in 1939, at the height of his success, he was stricken with a rare blood disease, agranulocytopenia, which is usually fatal, and from which he recovered very slowly. He had no sooner gotten over this than he was involved in World War II, conducting a scratch Navy band to tour South Pacific bases.

When Ava met him, Artie had returned from the war a

shattered man. The long tour of the back blocks of Australia had affected his nerves, and he was undergoing intensive psychoanalytical care under the specialist May Romm. Even before his illness, his disastrous marriages —including one to Lana Turner—and the decline of his personal fortunes, he had been savage, driving, uncompromising. Now his psychologically injured condition and that ultimate tragedy for a musician, encroaching deafness, made him more nervous and overwrought than ever. His hunger for women was constant, but it was impelled as much by a need to dominate and instruct as it was to make love to them.

"Artie went straight for the throat," the Hollywood producer Jack Sher says. "He had a fantastic, infallible technique with women. He would be warmly admiring, impress them with his intelligence, and they would be undermined by his handsome face and figure. Just as they were putting up the last defenses, he'd say, 'You're wonderful, there's absolutely nothing wrong with you EXCEPT ONE THING!' No woman could escape after that. She *had* to know what that one thing was if it killed her.

"In Ava's case, clearly, the thing was her sense of insecurity, her feeling of being out of her depth in a star career. Artie showed her how to fix that up. He got her into analysis. She went to *his* analyst, and no doubt all three exchanged notes."

Captivated by Ava's beauty, Artie was clearly determined to force her up to his intellectual level. Like many show business figures, he was a man who felt that the one thing he could not buy was intellectual respectability. He set out with an extraordinary degree of determination, the same degree he brought to his performance, to read and study to the point at which he could converse with the learned. He did not entirely succeed—a fact which no doubt added to his extreme frustration.

After several dates, Artie and Ava became seriously

involved emotionally and made almost immediate plans to marry. But from the outset their relationship was a disaster.

In the first place, Ava had read only one book from cover to cover: *Gone with the Wind*. Yet Shaw constantly pressed her to read.

Writer Nunnally Johnson remembers: "When Artie was playing at the Paramount Theater in New York during their honeymoon, Ava slipped away during a rehearsal, took a subway to the Times Building, and bought the current best-seller, *Forever Amber*, by Kathleen Winsor. She rushed back to show it to Artie. 'I *bought* a book!' she said. He went red in the face, snatched it from her, and threw it down a corridor. 'If I ever catch you reading shit like that again, I'll throw you out!' She stood shocked almost into tears. After their divorce, she had great pleasure in telling me, 'You've no idea what I just heard on the radio, Nunnally. That son-of-a-bitch just married Kathleen Winsor!' "

Scenes between them were frequent. When Artie gave Ava serious works of literature to read she did not understand them. This upset him badly. Back in Los Angeles, she decided to take a course in English literature to please him. She also took economics, both courses at UCLA. She sat in class—which was notably unsettled by her presence, the boys staring openly and their girlfriends visibly jealous—earnestly listening to the lectures.

After several crises, with their relationship almost over, Ava and Artie were suddenly married by Judge Stanley Mosk at his home at 1112 South Peck Drive, Beverly Hills, on the evening of October 17, 1945, with Frances Heflin as bridesmaid and Artie's close friend Hy Craft as best man. Ava wore almost exactly the same outfit she had worn at her wedding to Mickey two and a half years before: a blue tailored suit with a corsage of orchids.

After the wedding, the couple held a reception at the house with only a handful of guests, including Artie's mother Sara, Bappie, the Crafts, and the Heflins. They moved at once into a house on Bedford Drive. But the English-style manor house wasn't large enough for both of them, and their quarrels were lacerating.

The misery of Ava's second marriage was again based on the fact that the couple simply had nothing in common. It became a sadomasochistic hell for both of them, he tormenting her with her ignorance, she torturing him with her simple-hearted possessiveness. She was wracked by her feeling of inferiority, sensing that all she had to hold Artie was her beauty. This intensified her feeling that all she could hold audiences, too, with, was her beauty, that she was absolutely devoid of brains, wit, and the talent that should qualify a star. Artie became her audience, every man rolled into one. He worshipped her body and despised her brain: it was almost as though she had masochistically set out to create for herself a situation in which she could see the reality of her career under the most probing of domestic microscopes.

"I remember that awful marriage well," says Peggy Lloyd, wife of the actor and producer Norman Lloyd. "The Shaws came to my house at Malibu for a party. There was a woman there, a refugee, who had suffered terribly during the war. She had lost everything in Europe. She told her story at the party. Ava was deeply moved. In a sudden, typical gesture she took off the beautiful suede coat she was wearing and gave it to the woman, who burst into tears of gratitude. Artie screamed at Ava, what did she think she was doing giving away a beautiful coat to a stranger? There was a horrible scene. Ava had that simple, open generosity of a country girl. Artie hated her for it."

Ava's close friend Ruth Rosenthal (now Schechter)

says: "I also remember how horrible the relationship was. One night a group of us were at Artie's house, sitting around the living room floor. Ava was in a chair, with her shoes kicked off, and her bare feet tucked under her. Artie looked at her coldly and said in front of everyone, 'For God's sake, what are you doing? Do you think you're still in a tobacco field?' Well, she went white, she trembled, she cried. It was ghastly.

"She was acutely aware of her shortcomings. Even as late as 1945 she still kept the $10 coat and bobbysox she first came to Hollywood in to remind her of her humble origins. She was terrified of getting 'starry,' she was afraid of stardom itself. She would always want me on the set of a picture, the director would arrange it so she could see me there, to give her confidence. Before a particularly difficult scene, or before an interview, she would lie awake all night, just ill with terror. She went through hell.

"She was so desperately in need of love and attention. She talked constantly of her mother, and how her mother had suffered for years from breast cancer before she died, and Ava had sat beside her. She blamed herself for leaving her mother to go to New York when she first had the pictures taken by Larry Tarr.

"She was terrified not only of making movies but of the press. One night at a party someone made the mistake of turning on a radio, and the radio commentator—that infamous Louella Parsons—said Ava was in a love nest in Palm Springs. Well, Ava looked ill, desperate. I understood for the first time the horror she had of the press. She kept telling us all obsessively that Louella was wrong, that in fact she was right here in Benedict Canyon, not in Palm Springs. As if we didn't know!

"No matter what she said or did it came out badly in the press. She gave herself too generously to everyone. I remember once I went to Chicago and the plane was delayed on the way back. She stayed all night at the airport until 5 a.m. to meet me.

"People hurt that sweet girl constantly. It was because of the fear and hurt she went through that she first started drinking. I remember it was in 1946. She had never drunk more than sherry or beer before. Then one night she said she was going to mix Scotch and beer. Horrible. She mixed it, with an air of bravado, and it made her sick. But I think it eased her pain, and she stuck with it after that."

Ava was still studying at UCLA when, early in 1946, she learned that she was to be offered a starring role in a film based on Ernest Hemingway's famous short story *The Killers*. The producer Walter Wanger and his wife Joan Bennett had seen *Whistle Stop* and had been sufficiently impressed by Ava's talent to recommend her to Mark Hellinger, scheduled to produce *The Killers* at Universal.

At the time he bought the property with Hemingway's and the studio's enthusiastic endorsement, Hellinger was overworked, overweight, and short-tempered. His wife, the ex-Follies star Gladys Glad, tried to calm him, but it was impossible. The film was to launch him at Universal; he had a percentage of the gross profits. He was near-hysterical, consumed by an inner demon, a perfect candidate for the heart attack which killed him shortly afterward. He drove his team relentlessly.

Hellinger was looking for unknowns to add authenticity to the picture, and he had just cast a husky newcomer called Burt Lancaster, then under contract to Hal B. Wallis, as the killer Swede whom two men come to a small New Jersey town to shoot down. Opposite Lancaster, he needed a girl to play the role of Kitty, a beauti-

ful and treacherous gang moll whose constant lying
makes life difficult for the insurance investigator (Edmond O'Brien) sent to unravel the facts surrounding
Swede's death.

A number of well-known actresses had begged for the
role. But as soon as Hellinger ran *Whistle Stop* he called
Ava's agent, Charles Feldman. As she walked into his
office at Universal, he became more and more excited.
And the high-strung, irritable man attracted Ava's admiration and respect at once. Hellinger paced around the
room throwing off ideas like electric sparks, whipping her
out of her indifference. Their rapport was instant and
complete. She adored his energy and enthusiasm, and he
responded to her wry humor, her cynicism and slangy
obscene conversation.

Ava told Joe Hyams: "Mark saw me as an actress, not
as a sexpot. He trusted me from the beginning, and I
trusted him. I knew he was a genius. He gave me a
feeling of the responsibility of being a movie star which I
had never for a moment felt before." And this was no
manufactured quote, put in her mouth by a press agent:
she said as much to friends over and over again in the
months that followed.

On studio instructions Hellinger made a test of Ava in
a love scene with Lancaster. She was so perfectly convincing in her simulated passion that he called the test off
halfway through. He had absolute confidence in her.
After the humiliation she had suffered with Artie, this
boost to her ego came at precisely the right psychological
moment. Ava wept with joy as she flung her arms around
Bappie and told her the news. And her remark to Hellinger when she heard the studio executives approved her
test was classic: "Oh that's fantastic! And you know I
have even better news. I just got a B-plus in an exam for
English literature at UCLA!"

Then it seemed that the whole new venture would have to be called off: M-G-M was refusing to release her. She became apoplectic, shouting at everyone at Metro that she must be released, but it was only when Hellinger offered a record sum for her services that M-G-M reluctantly released her for the one picture.

Ava was delighted with her German director, the intelligent and forthright Robert Siodmak. Siodmak was infinitely patient with her, working for hours on her thin and watery voice, teaching her to convey deceitfulness and evasiveness and fear by subtle movements of the eyes. Seeing her limitations as an actress, he worked carefully to exploit her narrow range, and skillfully moved her into stardom.

Edmond O'Brien, still a close friend of Ava's, remembers how each morning Siodmak, bubbling humorously in his weirdly fractured English, would gather everyone together and then charge them with a fierce excitement. O'Brien says: "We were all new—Burt, Ava, and me; Siodmak and Hellinger gave us a feeling of being part of something important and a sense of what we could do with a scene that gave us extraordinary confidence. We all became fast friends. Siodmak would give each actor a key word: to me, 'inscrutable,' to Ava, 'smiling—but not smiling,' and so on. He taught us to convey emotion with the absolute minimum of facial expression. 'The camera is a magnifying glass,' he would say. He was so excited by Ava he let her dominate scene after scene. In a sequence in which the members of the gang were playing poker, he focused the camera entirely on her boredom and restlessness, which she most subtly conveyed, against a window drenched in a sudden downpour of rain. Her biggest scene was in the Green Cat Cafe when I needled her over and over again to tell the truth about a crime and she expressed terror. Siodmak told her to 'cut her expression in half' and to move her mouth slightly as she moved her eyes. She obeyed him totally, with the result that she gave a convincing account of a deceiving woman who is about to be caught.

"Siodmak pulled Ava and Burt and me up to concert pitch," O'Brien says. "When he was ill one day and a substitute was brought in to direct we all somehow lost our grip."

Years later, owlishly bespectacled in a house in Ascona, Switzerland, the late Robert Siodmak remembered Ava: "She was a very ignorant girl. Once at dinner we were drinking champagne, which she called shampoo. She thought that the wine was imported from France but that the bubbles were added in America. She drank champagne like Coca-Cola.

"She had already been in three or four movies before *The Killers* but none of them were any good. Certainly she had not displayed any talent in them. But I think that *The Killers* was the first part where she was really noticed. There was one scene in the picture which I was very worried about. I thought she might not be able to do it. That's the scene toward the end when she gets hysterical. Every day on the set I would tell her, 'If you don't do that scene right I shall *hit* you, I shall *kill* you.' My intention was to frighten her. We shot this particular scene toward the end of the shooting. Every day for five weeks I would make her nervous about that scene. On the day we had to shoot the scene I looked at her like Frankenstein's monster and I said, 'Ava, if you don't do this scene right, I shall *hit* you, I shall *kill* you.' She was so frightened by then that she really did get hysterical and she did the scene perfectly on the very first take. But it took me five weeks to prepare her for that scene."

The Killers won Ava excellent notices. She even earned the approval of Ernest Hemingway himself and of John

Huston, who wrote the screenplay under the counter because, he says, "I was in the Army and felt that a film
credit might suggest to my superiors that I was not devot-
ing all of my time to the job. I gave my collaborator,
Anthony Veiller, sole credit instead." Critics noted that
for the first time, Ava was capable of expressing emotions
with all of the skill of a fine actress. In her biggest scene,
she pleaded desperately with a dying Albert Dekker to
clear her name. She expressed boredom, aggression, insecurity, and terror with far more emotion than she had
hitherto shown, managing to compete successfully with the
intensity of the young Burt Lancaster, the toughness of
Edmond O'Brien, and the effortless playing of Dekker.
The lighting of her face by cameraman Norbert Brodine
was expert, helping to suggest deceitfulness by constantly
shadowing the eyes to conceal their expression. Hellinger
and Siodmak, like Moguy, taught her not to pose emptily,
as she had done in the M-G-M pictures, but to look into
herself for emotions she had once felt: fear, anxiety, hatred.
Though she was not a natural actress, she at least had managed to give the solid, authoritative impression of a coming
star, and she won the *Look* Award as the most promising
newcomer of 1947 as a result.

By the midsummer of 1946, Ava and Artie were no
longer sleeping in the same bed. Ava slept on a couch in
the living room. He was working all night and she was
working all day, so the move from one room to another
was really little more than a technicality.

Ava told a close friend in June that she and Artie had
not had sex for months. Some nights Ava moved out and
stayed with a variety of friends. Meanwhile, she continued to work at her courses at UCLA and to see her—
as well as Shaw's—analyst. She told a friend, "Everyone
in Hollywood has read at least *Ivanhoe*. They're talking

about filming it at Metro, and I haven't even opened a copy. I'm glad it's a set text in my course."

Shaw's interest in her had waned to the point that he didn't care if she came home and recited Shakespeare. Later that summer, she moved into the house of Minna Wallis, a gifted agent who was the sister of producer Hal B. Wallis. She began dating Howard Hughes again on and off, but most of the time she stayed at home studying and listening to the radio.

After her great success in *The Killers*, Ava was a household word. But she still dressed so casually that she was seldom recognized in public. Reporter Pete Martin wrote in the *Saturday Evening Post*: "Recently, she went to her bank to make a withdrawal. She wore shoulder-length red-brown hair all helter-skelter. She wore her favorite costume: saddle shoes and bobbysox, a ballerina skirt, a blouse. Her face was innocent of makeup. The cashier looked at her suspiciously, then retired to the back of the bank to check her signature and consult with the cashier. When he came back he said, 'I'm sorry, but you didn't look like Ava Gardner.'"

On August 16, after 10 months of marriage, she filed quietly for divorce in the Los Angeles Superior Court. She charged cruelty and made almost no demands on Shaw's property, asking only for the return of some possessions of hers that were still in the house. Her complaint said that she had experienced "grievous mental suffering," and that Shaw had treated her "cruelly." Deeply depressed—more so than she had been after the collapse of her marriage with Mickey—she began to talk about retiring from the screen for good. She told the *Los Angeles Times*: "What good will money and fame do me if I have no happy home? And money and fame is all that the studios and agents, who persuade me to stay in pictures, promise me." She felt an overwhelming urge to have her contract at M-G-M broken and to get a doctorate at UCLA.

On October 25, the divorce from Artie became final. Ava told the *Los Angeles Times*: "Artie became utterly and completely selfish in the last months of our marriage. I was barely able to hold back my tears. He disregarded my smallest wish and he persisted in humiliating me every chance he got. If I remained silent when we were with friends he would say, 'Why don't you talk? Have you nothing to contribute to the conversation?' But when I tried to say something he would say, 'Shut up!' "

Superior Judge Henry R. Archbald granted the decree.

The direct result of Ava's artistic and commercial success in *The Killers* was the more respectful treatment she received on her return to Metro. The smooth and civilized producer Arthur Hornblow, Jr., offered her almost at once a chance to co-star with Clark Gable and Deborah Kerr—who had just been imported from England— in the film version of Frederick Wakeman's advertising novel, *The Hucksters*. "We felt she would be a marvelous foil for Deborah," Hornblow says. "We were right."

At first Gable had refused to take the part at all. He had been disgusted by his comeback picture, *Adventure*, with Greer Garson (announced by the notorious slogan "Gable's Back and Garson's Got Him") and told Hornblow, "The novel is filthy and it isn't even entertainment." He agreed to appear in the film only after certain changes were made: the feminine lead in the story could not be married, as Gable would not tolerate acting an affair with a married woman, and the character of Kimberly, an anxious advertising executive, must be deprived of the satyriasis—an uncontrollable sexual urge—which burdened him in the book. Moreover, Gable would not accept the fact that the character he played failed to strike

back at the advertising boss who humiliated him. He
insisted on a scene in which he emptied a pitcher of water
over the superior's bald head.

The part she was offered—a good-natured singer who
is cast off by the hero—scarcely appealed to Ava. But the
opportunity of acting with Gable was far too inviting to
miss. When she had first come to Hollywood she had seen
him in a car passing her in San Fernando Valley and had
stared at him so hard she had almost crashed. Now,
meeting him, she was completely overawed.

He turned out to be extremely considerate and helpful.
He told her, "You don't see yourself as an actress and I
don't see myself as an actor. That makes us even." Between scenes of *The Hucksters*, he offered her his star
chair and lit her cigarettes. When she fluffed, which was
often, he patiently accepted her nervousness and in a
break quietly told her how to improve a line. She was
particularly frightened of playing a love scene with him.
By the time it came along, she was so bamboozled at
meeting the chalk line, making sure her hair and costume
were perfect, and noting where photographer Harold
Rosson told her to look, she forgot every word she was
supposed to say, and the director, Jack Conway, bawled
her out unmercifully.

Off set, Gable was unattracted to her. He talked to
her about his fondness for spending four months of each
year fishing and hunting or working his ranch. He talked
constantly of Carole Lombard. He talked of his plans to
remake *Red Dust*, the picture that had obsessed her as a
child. Asked by a reporter from *Movie Show* magazine in
what she would like to star with Gable, she said unhesi-
tatingly, "In the Harlow role in *Red Dust*!" (Six years
later she would get her wish.)

To Ava's astonishment, Gable fluffed his lines the second day of shooting, throwing her completely. Jack Con-

way was very nervous, shouting "Cut—please Clark, let's do it again!" at the end of each scene. The retakes were endless for one short sequence, and by lunchtime nothing had been printed at all. Ava fled to her dressing room and started to cry.

Gable suddenly appeared, benign and reassuringly fatherly, in the doorway. He said, "I'm sorry, Ava. I loused everything up. The truth is, I wasn't thinking about what I was saying, I was so darn worried about you." He paused a moment. "I was scared you wouldn't live up to my hopes for you. But you're okay, kiddo!" And he shook her hand.

When Gable gave a radio interview in which he commented on Ava's excellence and very real promise, she made arrangements to have a transcript disc sent to her: she spent evenings at her apartment in Westwood playing it over and over again.

During the last stages of shooting *The Hucksters*, Arthur Hornblow received a frantic telephone call from Jerry Bresler, producer of a new Universal-International melodrama, *Singapore*. He needed a leading woman in a hurry because his female star had gotten ill. Could Ava possibly start work at once without having completed her scenes in *The Hucksters?*

Hornblow reluctantly agreed to help Universal out of a jam. Ava had to drive from M-G-M to Universal each day. On her first scene, she switched dresses in a matter of minutes and rushed onto the set representing a steamy tropical room, where she was told to walk up to Fred MacMurray and yield to a passionate embrace. Her only insistence was that she use nothing but street makeup and a little powder. Bresler was not in a position to argue.

Despite the fact that she had barely any time to read the script of *Singapore*, Ava somehow managed to grasp the essentials of her role of a woman suffering from amnesia. To add to her problems, Roland Culver, the British actor, had also been rushed into his part at a moment's notice; the two of them had considerable difficulty giving a degree of conviction to their scenes as husband and wife. Ava was also disconcerted by director John Brahm's habit of listening to shortwave radio from Singapore with the aid of his sound recording engineer, Martin Brown, to pick up some more touches of "local color." In one scene, Brahm failed to warn her when George Lloyd, playing a sinister homosexual villain, struck her in the face with an expensive string of pearls. The pearls broke, scattering all over the sound stage, and a moment later she was on all fours looking for them.

They had to shoot some scenes at four o'clock in the morning because up to that time the bullfrogs on the backlot kept up an *obbligato* to her dialogue. She also had to leave for Palmdale to shoot scenes at an airfield at dawn.

The worst moment of all came during the shooting of a fire sequence. Without warning part of a burning ceiling caved in, narrowly missing her. A burning spar of wood did hit Fred MacMurray, setting fire to his white tropical suit. He ran over to the fire squad, which managed to douse him in time.

Director Brahm says: "I remember little about that picture, but I do remember Ava very well. She didn't have a brain in her head. She was just a nice girl who was trying very hard. When one scene was over she'd sit down and start talking with her sister about cooking and husbands and knitting. I don't think she had any interest in being a film star at all."

Made in a rush, *Singapore* was a flop, but *The Hucksters*, also released in 1947, greatly aided Ava's career. Although Bosley Crowther of *The New York Times* gave her a bad time, many other critics expressed admiration of her playing and predicted a great future for her.

She was handed over to Ann Straus for another grueling series of photographs. During one harrowing month, more than 900 Gardner photographs were taken in 62 changes of clothing, with accessories to match, and in an enormous variety of makeups.

During this period, Ava had been virtually dateless, aside from some infrequent, rather unstimulating visits with Howard Hughes. In the fall of 1947, soon after completing *Singapore*, she made a trip to New York for promotion of *The Killers* in the company of Mark Hellinger. One evening, Hellinger called her at her hotel and told her that a personable young Universal contract actor, Howard Duff, was in New York for the first time to make *The Naked City*, didn't know anybody, and wondered if she would like to have a date. "Put him on the line," she drawled. She liked Duff's voice—he sounded amusing and lighthearted—and she went out with him that night.

Hellinger's publicist Frank McFadden set up the arrangements for the date. Howard Duff was to pick Ava up at the Plaza. "I'll never forget when Howard went to collect Ava," McFadden says. "She came down the steps, with fans gaping at her, and amateur photographers rushing up to take pictures, and I think she expected to be greeted at the bottom by an expensively dressed film star in an enormous shiny limousine.

"Instead, Howard was driving a beaten-up jalopy that looked like a battered tank, and he was dressed in jeans, loafers, and a shabby old jacket. Well, when she realized he was her date for the evening she yelled! With laughter! She loved the incongruity of it all, and she loved Howard for not putting on the dog!"

She was immediately attracted to him. He in his turn

says: "Even though I was going with Yvonne DeCarlo at the time I met Ava, I had long carried a torch for her. When I saw her, she seemed like the most beautiful thing I had ever seen. I was crazy about her, infatuated with her. My male ego told me, 'Get her if it kills you.' "

I interviewed Howard Duff in 1973, in the raffish, sea-green gloom of the Beverly Hills Hotel's Polo Lounge. Heavier by then, his face fringed with grizzled sideburns, Duff still was a charmer, a brash, uncomplicated, aggressively masculine extrovert TV star who, unlike most actors, was modest and correctly judged his own level of acting. He told me: "It was quite a night. We went to Greenwich Village for a fish dinner. Then we went from nightclub to nightclub, getting sloshed all the way. She was incredibly restless. If we were in one place, she wanted to be in another. She was never satisfied. Quickly I understood how mercurial and changeable she was, maddening, exasperating one minute, adorable the next, a mixture of qualities that baffled and infuriated me. But sexually she had me hooked at the outset.

"I went back to Hollywood after that first night and I didn't see her for months. But I was already drunk with her, and I broke with Yvonne for her."

When Ava next met Howard Duff the attraction resumed with even greater intensity, and their love affair began. Duff says: "We had a restless, volatile relationship. What did we have in common? Ava. No, that isn't fair. We were both immature, we both liked to do very little reflecting, we never wanted to read. But the main difference between us was that I liked to live fairly quietly, whereas she always wanted to be doing something so she wouldn't have to sit still. And think.

"We went to nightclubs constantly, especially Ciro's. She was a night person. But when she was working she disciplined herself completely. She liked to give the impression that she didn't care about her roles, but she was in fact pretty damn serious and dedicated. I had to drive her home early. She was always first at the studio into makeup. She drove herself without mercy.

"Her humor specialized in put-downs. I must say she frequently used put-downs on me. She did everything in fits and starts. She'd start one thing, stop it, and start another. I remember we went all the way to La Quinta, near Palm Springs, to take tennis lessons from a pro she'd heard about. After a day Ava got tired of that. Every day she'd change from mood to mood—so fast nobody, least of all me, could keep up with her. We'd laugh and have fun and then we'd have terrible, terrible quarrels and throw things. She could be very violent—she once hit Howard Hughes in the teeth with a candlestick.

"She was like Carole Lombard: she used profanity worse than anyone I ever knew. Gradually I came to understand that although she thought she wanted one husband, one home, for a long period, in fact she wasn't meant to devote her life to one person at all. I also began to realize that she didn't feel about me the way I felt about her.

"And we ran out of things to do. I remember one night when we'd done everything, she said, 'Why don't we get the blender and put everything in the house into it, and mix it up?' So I got the blender and mixed it and mixed it—vodka, gin, Scotch, brandy, you name it. It was fantastic—and *whammo!* We were 'out' on the carpet."

During 1948, Ava was frequently at Ciro's with Howard Duff. Others in the "gang" were Lana Turner, Ava's new roommate—a swinging blonde called Peggy Maley—and Ann Sheridan and their various handsome dates.

Ciro's ex-boss Herman Hover remembers: "I think only Lana, of all the partying stars, could keep up with her pace. Sometimes she and Lana would just take off to

Mexico and fling parties down there. They hated to sleep
at night, and Ava wouldn't rest. She loved to drink a lot,
but she wasn't a lush, I never saw her drunk, and when
she was on a picture I never saw her at all."

Aside from Duff, Ava dated the bandleader at Ciro's,
Jerry Wald (not to be confused with the producer), and
(again) Peter Lawford. Duff says: "Robert Walker also
took her out a few times—and he was a tragic alcoholic.
When he tried to beat her up I would like to have
creamed him—only he was so helpless."

The affair with Duff, more important than any of these
temporary liaisons, continued through 1948 and 1949,
while Ava moved from apartment to apartment, from
Westwood to Beverly Hills or Fountain Avenue in Hollywood and back again, sometimes sharing her home with
Peggy Maley, sometimes with her maid Mearene Jordan,
sometimes with Bappie, but always afraid of being alone
when Howard was not with her.

In 1948, she made another film for Universal, *One
Touch of Venus*, playing the part of a department store
statue of Venus which comes to life when Robert Walker
kisses it.

(When Universal asked for her for the film, Metro
again refused to let her go. She personally begged Louis
B. Mayer to let her work there. She was told she was
needed at once to make a new melodrama, *The Bribe*.
But fortunately, this film was delayed, making her available.)

Robert Walker was cast as the floorwalker, Dick
Haymes as his roommate, and Tom Conway as the department store boss, with Eve Arden as Conway's cynical
secretary. William A. Seiter directed. Ava responded to
Seiter's direction with a witty and self-mocking great
style and charm.

Ava's flowing robes for the role were so nearly trans-
parent that a special assistant had to follow her around

with a portable heater. She posed in a swimsuit for an Italian sculptor, who told her he could not proceed unless she removed the covering from her breasts. "Sure that's enough?" she said cheerfully as she pulled off the top half of her swimsuit and rolled down the lower half until it resembled the thinnest of bikinis.

Ava worked on the part of Venus with a ruthless drive that astounded director Seiter. Her casualness gone, she worked all day and well into the night with dance director Billy Daniels to perfect her steps. Ava's chief relaxation was when Howard Duff dropped by to have lunch with her in her dressing room. When people knocked at her door, Howard would answer through it, "This is Ava here" in his deep baritone voice, and he and Ava would fall over in laughter.

Despite its bad reviews, *One Touch of Venus* was a very good movie, marred only by its low budget and its black-and-white modesty of format. Ava was excellent in the all-important part of the Anatolian Venus. At once witty, tender, and intensely, startlingly sensual, she was the epitome of sex and a living mockery of seduction. Considering her lack of experience in comedy, she showed a surprising command of timing. And she had never looked more beautiful, her profile alone establishing her claim to be as classic a goddess as Venus herself.

After *One Touch of Venus*, Ava returned to Metro to make the long postponed *The Bribe*. Pandro Berman, its producer, says today: "We should never have made that heap of junk. It was a lousy picture and everyone was terrible in it. We had a rotten script we couldn't lick—we kept changing it, finally adding a flashback structure, but it still didn't work. We sat in the cutting room for days but it still stank. Mercifully, I've blocked out most of it. It went off on the assembly line and was forgotten. As it deserved."

An imitation of Warner Brothers' recent hit with

Bogart and Bacall, *To Have and Have Not, The Bribe*
was a steamy melodrama directed by a man wholly unsuited to this type of subject: the roly-poly Robert Z.
Leonard, who had directed Nelson Eddy-Jeanette Mac-
Donald musicals. "Ava was notably ill-at-ease all the time
she was on the set," cameraman Joe Ruttenberg remembers. "No wonder. She only smiled when Howard Duff
dropped by for a joke or two."

Ava by this time had developed a horror of Metro and
the wretched parts it persisted in giving her; *The Bribe*,
despite the presence in the cast of such stalwarts as
Charles Laughton and John Hodiak, was among the
worst pictures she ever made.

Still moving from apartment to apartment, changing
her telephone number weekly, still dating several men,
still on the nightclub circuit, and often showing the results in her tired, puffy-eyed, and haggard look on the
screen, Ava was still refusing after a year to marry Howard Duff. The truth was that though she enjoyed his
company very much, though she found him an agreeably
tough, shrewd, and amusing companion, this longest of
all of her affairs outside of marriage was not really a love
relationship. It was a friendship of which the physical
affair was merely a part. Duff says: "I was obsessed with
Ava, as any red-blooded man would be. Often I wanted
to beat her, she was so maddening. Often I hated her,
more often I adored her. But I knew in my heart she
never loved me."

It was during this period—according to one of her
closest women friends—that a horrifying episode occurred. Ava became pregnant and decided to have an
abortion. She went to an unqualified doctor in Beverly
Hills on a Saturday morning. He operated on her without
an anesthetic so that she would understand the magnitude
of what she was doing. He botched the job, not com-

pletely removing the fetus. The aftermath was appalling. Her womb was so badly cut that it probably would have been very difficult for her to have any children. The event so traumatized her that she never fully recovered from the shock, and never had a child.

Eve Arden, Ava's friend and comedy co-star in *One Touch of Venus*, remembers Ava after this incident: "I had adopted three children, and Ava used to come to my house on Outpost Drive to see them. She adored them, and I always felt she was in a state of anguish because she didn't—or couldn't—have children of her own.

"She was drinking quite heavily, and since I was a teetotaler I found this mildly shocking at that time. But I adored her and it didn't upset me too much.

"She had put down quite a bit of absinthe when she decided to go swimming in my pool. I lent her one of my bathing suits and I was terrified that it might come off since I was so much bigger, or that with all the absinthe in her she might drown! I know that when she looked at the children there was an intense sadness in her eyes. And then she drank some more absinthe. But she went in the pool and swam beautifully!"

Later in 1948, Ava was cast in yet another dull Metro movie, *The Great Sinner*, based on the novel *The Gambler* by Dostoevski. The story was set in the Wiesbaden Casino in the 1880s, brilliantly designed by the art director Hans Peters.

Ava was cast as the daughter of a Russian general. Opposite her, Gregory Peck was cast as Fedja—based on Dostoevski himself—whose compulsion for gambling almost brings about his ruin.

The script's co-author, Christopher Isherwood, was seriously upset by the miscasting of Peck and Ava, and the director, Robert Siodmak, refused later to admit he had directed the picture at all. "Mervyn LeRoy did all of it," he says. Mervyn LeRoy's comment is: "I never heard of *The Great Sinner*. That Siodmak guy was crazy!"

During the making of *The Great Sinner* Ava's informality achieved legendary status at the studio. During the lunch break, while the other stars remained aloof in their dressing rooms, she wandered among the crew, sharing chicken and hot dogs with them.

Producer George Edwards, who was then a young extra, remembers her vividly: "A group of us were sitting, bored, between scenes, in groups on the edge of the sound stage, wearing our heavy period costumes. She walked by in a magnificent black ball dress with a skirt that seemed to billow for miles around her. I'd heard she'd gotten a swollen head, that she was 'starry' and 'uppity.' Instead, she laughed as she saw us staring at her in a daze, and suddenly without warning she pulled her skirts up as far as they would go. We all had a look, naturally. Well, she had *jeans* on, under the skirts! She laughed again. 'You see,' she said, 'that's what the gorgeous Ava Gardner really is!' "

Cameraman George Folsey says: "Ava acted casual, it's true. She behaved like the farm girl she was, without any pretense. The first day she came on the set, I thought, 'Oh, she won't know anything.' Then she came up to me and said, 'Hello, George. You know I like only reflected light on my face, and a small spotlight under my chin!' I nearly fell over!"

Folsey adds: "She had extraordinary patience under Bob Siodmak. He'd take a scene scores of times just because some tiny detail of dress nobody would notice was wrong. One day he'd done about sixty takes of her. And she said, very nicely, right in front of the cast, 'Bob? Do you think I could go to the bathroom after the eighty-first take?' "

By late 1948, Ava positively refused to take her new-found star status seriously. She delivered a self-revealing contradiction to a fan magazine reporter who visited her on the *Great Sinner* set: "Deep down," she said, "I'm pretty superficial."

Also by late 1948, Ava had become more and more depressed by apartment living, and after two moves, settled on buying a pretty cottage high up in Nichols Canyon in Hollywood. Drenched in sunlight, painted a vivid Mediterranean yellow, it seemed ideal for her purposes. She and her maid Mearene, who was an amateur painter, moved in and began working on the decoration during the last weekends of shooting. It was a joy to have her own home at last, and she splurged at auctions—one particular set of antique silver made a sizable dent in her bank balance—and bought solid walnut bookshelves, crowding the walls with her large collection of books. She ran around in jeans and a check shirt rolled up at the elbows, painting the bedroom, helping the deliverers put down the string carpet, decorating the den in cocoa wood. Work on the garden was tough: the soil was sandy or rocky and resistant, and there were patches of stone on the hillside.

But it was an individual and attractive house, alive with contrasts of color, the walls sparkling with Ava's collection of vivid Degas ballet prints. And during late 1948, Ava was happier than she had been in several years. When they didn't quarrel violently, the affair with Howard Duff was lighthearted and pleasant, she enjoyed the company of Mearene, and she spent many evenings sitting on the floor barefoot or in loafers listening to her collection of classical and popular records. It was wonderful to escape from the heavy fustian lines of *The Great Sinner* script and relax completely.

With George Raft in *Whistle Stop* (UNITED ARTISTS)

Left: With Burt Lancaster in *The Killers* (UNIVERSAL). *Opposite*: Dancing with Artie Shaw at the Hollywood Mocambo (WIDE WORLD PHOTOS)

At ringside with Howard Hughes during a Joe Louis
heavyweight match (UNITED PRESS INTERNATIONAL PHOTO)

Above: Clark Gable, Ava Gardner, Deborah Kerr, Gloria Holden,
Adolphe Menjou in *The Hucksters* (M-G-M). *Below*: Clark Gable,
Ava Gardner, Edward Arnold in *The Hucksters* (M-G-M)

Ava Gardner in *One Touch of Venus* (UNIVERSAL)

Above: With Walter Huston, Melvyn Douglas, and Gregory Peck in *The Great Sinner* (M-G-M). *Below*: With James Mason between the scenes of *East Side, West Side* (M-G-M)

Howard Duff escorting a startlingly blond Ava Gardner

In her Irene-designed bathing suit, with Robert Taylor in *The Bribe* (M-G-M)

In January 1949, Ava revisited Smithfield and posed
for pictures with the local mayor, who presented her with
the keys to the city. She also posed for a *Photoplay*
layout, sitting on the porch of her Brogden birthplace*—
the paint now in poor repair—and looking soulfully into
the middle distance for the cameras, her feet tucked
under her tomboyishly. Elsie Mae (now Mrs. D. L.
Creech) and Inez (Mrs. John A. Grimes) were comfortably fat and cheerful, posing reluctantly with their
lovely sister in the dining room of Elsie Mae's house. Ava
also romped on a sofa with her niece, Mary Edna
Grimes, 15, who had become so plump in the family
tradition that she could no longer get into Ava's castoffs.
Ava was surrounded by neighbors at a local store which
her father had once owned and which had passed into the
hands of Elsie Mae and her husband. She posed for a
family picture with her cousins and nephews and kept
everyone in an uproar with her Hollywood stories.

She flew away with her arms full of flowers to Hollywood—and Howard Duff.

Ava's career had taken a sharp downgrade with *The
Great Sinner*, and her next feature, *East Side, West Side*,
was scarcely a help. It was a smooth, glossy, and mean-
ingless Metro concoction, based on a successful novel by
Marcia Davenport about wealthy New Yorkers.

Ava delivered a few well-chosen vulgarities when she
read the script and discovered that yet again she was to
play a cast-off "other woman," a sleazier version of her
part in *The Hucksters*, and that she would again be called
upon to toss her hair sultrily, lean against pianos in black
satin with long gloves, and exude ersatz heavy-breathing
sex for reel after reel.

* She kept calling it by the nickname "Grabtown" in interviews.

"They could see I was good in comedy after *One Touch of Venus*, that I hated these miserable cast-off woman parts," she told a fan magazine reporter. "But they kept on making me the heavy." She more or less walked through her role, acting minimally. But she liked the peppery little director, Mervyn LeRoy. One day she said to him, "I've changed my psychiatrist." "Why?" he snapped back at her. "Because someone told me to." "Who?" "Another psychiatrist," she said, and they roared with laughter.

Shortly after the film was finished, Ann Straus traveled with Ava to Chicago to appear at a benefit performance of the picture with Keenan Wynn and Jackie Cooper. The original idea was to have Ava tell jokes and sing on stage. "In a mood of bravado," Ann says, "Ava agreed. But by the time we got to Chicago on the train she was sick with fear. She knew she had no talent for telling funny stories and she was desperately insecure about singing in public, or in fact doing *anything* on a stage. By the time we arrived she had been to the bathroom 100 times in three days. Before she was due to hit the stage she drank several straight bourbons, and even then I had to push her on the stage with the flat of my hand. She stood there, whispered a few sweet nothings, and then fled. Luckily, the audience was on her side, and quite a few GIs were there to give her wolf whistles. But that was the end. 'Ann,' she said, 'I'll never appear on a stage again!' And she almost never did."

Promotion for *East Side, West Side* also involved going to a ranch in central California and posing in country clothes and swimsuits. As always, Ava hated the assignment, which was softened only by the fact that the very pleasant studio publicity woman went with her. The nights were agonies of boredom for Ava, following long and insufferable hours posing in clothes she didn't like.

One evening she said to Ann Straus, "I've got to swim." Ann said, "You can't! Look at the sign. No one in the pool after nine."

Ava was furious. "I want to go in!"

Ann shouted, "Ava you're NOT going in! Even if it weren't for the rules you know what the press would do with this. They'd say you got blind drunk and went into the pool naked!" Ann won.

Chapter 6

DURING THE LATE 1940s, Ava had frequently bumped into Frank Sinatra, either at M-G-M, where he had worked on some musicals, or at RKO, where he was making films at the same time she was filming a forgotten turkey under the aegis of Howard Hughes, *My Forbidden Past*.

According to Ruth (Rosenthal) Schechter: "Ava disliked Frank intensely. She kept saying that she found him conceited, arrogant, and overpowering. They had an instant hostility.

"I guess you could say this instant hostility was a precursor of a sudden romantic interest. In 1950, Ava attended a premiere of *Gentlemen Prefer Blondes* in New

York and ran into Frank in the lobby. She felt an over-powering attraction. The next day their meeting was the talk of New York."

Ava did not meet Frank again until two weeks latei at a party in Palm Springs. Once again, they felt a surge of mutual admiration; and on this occasion they felt much freer to express it. After the party, he drove her home in his car, stopping on the way to sing to her under a palm tree. The absurd, charming romantic gesture made them both laugh. Next day, they rode through nearby towns, Frank firing blanks from a revolver out of his car win-dow.

Their affair flourished quickly. Ava had dinner with Howard Duff and told him their own affair was com-pletely over, a fact he acknowledged gracefully. "I had known it was over weeks before," he says. "The truth is, that Ava was not at any stage interested in marrying me."

Mellow and assured today, and a success after his brief retirement, in 1950 Frank Sinatra was a hollow-chested, scrawny-limbed stringbean who looked as though a breeze would blow him over. His skull-like head, thinning black patent leather hair, absurdly exaggerated padded-shoulder zoot suits, and flopping rainbow-colored ties gave the im-pression of a walking, talking coat hanger. His appeal to women was due partly to his frankly sexual approach to songs—he would fling his thin legs wide, thrust his meager pelvis up into the spotlight glare—partly to his little-boy-lost look—they wanted to take care of him—and not least to his easy Latin charm. Ava had always found Latins, especially if they were thin, olive-skinned, hairy-chested, and volatile, very attractive. Frank was no exception. The fact that he was on his way to being a has-been at the time did not faze her.

Like Artie Shaw, Frank was heading downhill profes-sionally when he met Ava. His record sales were falling;

agents were having difficulty booking him into major night-spots. The affair with Ava was probably the best thing that happened to him in 1950; their intense, supercharged relationship gave drama and excitement to an otherwise depressing winter and early spring.

They were drawn to each other not only because of sexual attraction but because they were so much alike. Both were night people, barely capable of sleeping at all, liking to sit up into the small hours. Both loved Italian food, hard liquor, boxing matches; both were generous, warm, fiercely honest, violent-tempered, afraid of being used, deeply insecure and skeptical of their own talents, neurotic, tension-ridden. Their energies fused, and their relationship was from the outset passionate and yet deeply frustrating, tormenting because, similar as they were, they had a terrifying ability to seek out each other's weaknesses.

At the outset, Ava had the upper hand. Though not very talented, she was beginning to be established as a famous figure; though still a major talent, he was losing his grip, and it seemed that within five years he would be totally eclipsed. Ava's thwarted motherly instinct found new roots in a man undernourished, frightened, and desperate. She had a deep-seated urge to help him out of the mire.

Later, when she succeeded, when she helped push him back into the spotlight, he apparently began to resent her help. She now became the inferior. But her ego would not permit that. Much as she despised herself as an actress, she loved the power that a star's position gave her. It became intolerable to her that Frank should overpower her in the relationship.

In those puritanical days, their stormy affair became a public scandal. Frank had a wife, Nancy Sinatra, and three children. Louis B. Mayer complained bitterly to Ava about the unwelcome publicity the relationship was bringing to his studio, but his attitude merely sharpened her desire to be seen in public with Frank as often and as overtly as possible. Not that she wanted to force Frank to break with Nancy. But she knew that his feeling for her was far more intense than any he felt for Nancy, and that he found in her a far greater companionship of spirit.

Throughout the holiday season at the end of the year, the affair continued in Palm Springs and Hollywood. In January 1951, Frank invited Ava to join him at the Shamrock Hotel in Houston, Texas, where he was booked for a brief engagement. In order not to excite too much publicity in Hollywood, he and Ava left for Texas on separate planes. Frank went with his close friend, the songwriter Jimmy Van Heusen. As he was changing planes in El Paso, Frank received a phone call telling him that his press agent George Evans had died suddenly in the east. He canceled the first days of his engagement and flew to New York for the funeral, while Ava checked into a suite at the Shamrock alone.

The next week, the couple were happily reunited at the Shamrock and drove off to a dinner party at Vincent's Sorrento restaurant, with Mayor Oscar Holcombe as a host. When Edward Schisser, a photographer for the *Houston Press*, found out where they had gone, he came over to the table while they were eating spaghetti and asked Frank quietly if he might take their picture. Later, Frank said, "I refused graciously." The *Los Angeles Times* quoted Frank as saying, "No pictures with or without spaghetti." According to Schisser, he said, "Beat it, you bum." When Schisser did not move away, Frank leaped to his feet and looked like he was going to smash the camera and punch Schisser on the jaw. According to Schisser, Ava screamed and hid her face. The incident made headlines and embarrassed Ava.

After Texas, Frank was booked into the Copacabana

in New York for a brief engagement. It was his first important exposure for some time, and he was deeply afraid of failure. Ava traveled with him to New York, taking, for discretion's sake, a separate suite at the Hampshire House. On the first night, Frank was shaking, pale, and sweating before he went on stage. After doing everything she could to soothe him, Ava went out front and watched him closely, trying to throw support to him. But when he sang, apparently accidentally, "Nancy with a laughing face," the crowd turned and laughed at her. She brazened the scene out, but it badly unsettled her.

With a severe throat infection, and with nerves stretched to the limit, for he was aware that audiences were indifferent to him, Frank struggled through performance after performance. It was an ordeal which culminated in a grotesque and widely reported scene. One night, Ava, wearied by Frank's neuroses, went out with Artie Shaw and some other friends. Frank heard she was with Shaw and called various nightclubs until he found her. When he reached her he told her he was going to kill himself. He fired two shots, apparently into a mattress of his bed in the Hampshire House. She screamed and dropped the telephone, telling her party that she must go to the Hampshire House at once. She was in a state of hysteria all the way to the hotel, screaming and crying helplessly.

In the meantime, David O. Selznick, who was staying in the hotel, had heard the shots from Sinatra's neighboring suite and called the police. "I think the son-of-a-bitch shot himself," he said.

"I was staying there at the time," actor Tom Drake remembers. "Everyone in the hotel was talking about Ava and Frank and their love affair, and now this! The corridor was full of police, firemen, you never saw anything like it."

Ava, Artie and their friends arrived in the corridor and forced their way up to a cordon of police. Frank was obviously badly shaken. When the police finally left, the mattress had disappeared: apparently it was exchanged for another one and burned.

It was an agonizing period for Ava, and she was relieved to learn in March that she would be able to escape from the relationship for a time. Some months before, Albert Lewin, a tiny, partially deaf Metro director, had written a script called *Pandora and the Flying Dutchman*, a fantasy about an affair between a playgirl of the early 1930s and the Flying Dutchman of legend, who returns as a painter-yachtsman to Spain. Lewin cast James Mason as the Dutchman, and wrote the part of Pandora Reynolds, the tragic, flippant, willful playgirl, specifically for Ava.

The attraction of the role was that it would take her to Spain, a country she had always wanted to visit, and that it would give her some emotional respite. After an unhappy, nervous parting from Frank, she flew with Bappie to London on March 26, 1950, and transferred to a plane for Barcelona, where she stayed at the Sea Gull Inn until a suitable villa could be prepared for her.

Almost at once, Ava's relief at not being with Frank changed to a miserable loneliness. Telephone calls crossed the Atlantic as she lay sleepless each night, finding it hard to concentrate on details of her role. But Lewin forced her to work at her part with a degree of dedication and concentration. She showed that she understood the Surrealist implications of the part, and she impressed Lewin with her professional ease.

She fell in love with Spain. She loved the ocean location, the stretch of coast 80 miles north of Barcelona, and the solitary beaches south of the city near Sitges. In 1950, that area of the Costa Brava was almost untouched by tourism—it was a far cry from the crowded "Gold Coast" that it is today.

Mario Cabre was chosen by Lewin to play Ava's bull-fighter lover. He had acted only small roles in unimportant films, but he was then at the peak of his popularity as a bullfighter, even though he was a second-rate performer in the ring. His fame was a result of skillful self-advertisement in the press; he was frequently mentioned in the social columns for dating celebrated beauties. He wrote poetry—also second-rate—and often appeared on the radio. He was, to Ava, an ideal Latin type: proud, fierce, thin, tall by Spanish standards, dark-skinned, broad-shouldered and narrow-hipped. He dressed to perfection in dark suits with narrow elegant ties, and he had flawless manners, immense charm, a highly cultured line of conversation: in other words, he was the perfect escort and lover, but she never took him very seriously.

A Spanish friend of Cabre's says: "For Mario it was a chance to be a big star, for Ava it was a pleasant companionship. But it meant nothing to her, and if they had sex, it was only a very few times."

While in Barcelona, Ava learned that Frank had collapsed with a throat hemorrhage at the Copacabana, and was seriously ill. In defiance of doctor's orders, he flew to be with Ava on May 10, chartering a plane to fly him directly to Spain with Jimmy Van Heusen. He arrived in Barcelona gray and limp with sickness and exhaustion, and under 130 pounds. He was carrying a small parcel. The local reporters did everything in their power to find out its contents, but he refused to disclose what it was.

Ava greeted Frank passionately at the Sea Gull Inn, and opened the parcel, which contained an expensive bracelet. That night, dodging reporters, they slipped away for a long drive down the coast. As they returned, rain sprinkled the windshield. By the next day, a raging storm had completely canceled the preliminary shooting of the picture at Palamos and isolated the couple in a rented villa.

Frank was still exhausted from the flight, and his throat was like an open sore. Luckily, Cabre was out of town in Gerona, working on a sequence with the assistant director. While Frank fretted miserably, the press aggravated him by swarming outside the house and ringing the doorbell incessantly.

Even Ava's constant reassertions that Cabre meant absolutely nothing to her did not help. And when Cabre gave an interview to reporters from Madrid emphasizing again his passionate interest in Ava, Frank was close to apoplexy. He decided that he should never have come to Spain, and that the immense publicity attached to his visit would further affect his declining popularity. The rain continued to pour down, and there was only one brief break in which Frank managed to slip through the cordon and do some shopping in Tossa del Mar.

His parting from Ava was awkward and uncomfortable for both of them. The sheer unpleasantness of the trip, the rain, the fact that the press made them prisoners, Cabre's obstinate assertions of "love," made the whole period another nightmare following the horror of the Copacabana episode and the misery both had suffered in New York.

Just as Frank was leaving, Ava had word that she must immediately do a scene in the heart of Tossa del Mar, a scene in which Mario Cabre would appear as a triumphant matador receiving the ecstatic praise of his fans. The rain had cleared and the local Festival of San Ysidro made it convenient to use a large and excitable crowd. So as Frank's plane took off she was in the street, pushing through the crowd and shouting "Mario! Mario!" and

blowing Cabre kisses. Cabre smiled back and for a moment looked as though he would jump from his horse-
drawn carriage and take Ava in his arms. Once the scene
was over, he kissed her passionately in front of everyone
and said, "Hello, baby." Then he bared his chest to the
mob and said, "This is where a bull gored me yesterday. I
was distracted by my feeling for Ava. I think of her day
and night. She is sublime." That night, he and Ava were
reunited—"for dinner," as reporters discreetly said.

Frank flew back to his family in Los Angeles.

Once again Ava wanted to be reunited with Frank, and
so the extreme slowness of the director was a torment. He
would take hours over one setup, arranging her as carefully as an ornament. His deafness also was something of
an irritation.

James Mason too was somewhat ill-at-ease with Lewin.
"It's because he was deaf," Mason says today. "He lacked
a sense of the pulse of life."

Back in California, Sinatra was as taciturn as ever
about his affair with Ava. Asked by the *Los Angeles
Times* how Ava felt about him, he snapped, "I never got
around to asking her." With the many presents he had
bought at Tossa del Mar, Paris, and London, he drove off
to his house in Holmby Hills, spent a few hours of the
evening and one night at home with Nancy and the children, then flew to New York with a group of people that
included Bob Hope. Two days later, on May 26, Ava flew
to London from Barcelona and denied having any romantic involvement with Cabre. As for Frankie, she
"would rather not say anything." She said, correctly, that
she had had no telephone calls, cables, or letters from
him since he went home. She began working on pickup
sequences and special interiors at M-G-M's British studios,
and moved into a handsome apartment in Park Lane.

On July 10, Frank flew into London and moved into a

lavishly furnished apartment in Berkeley Square for two months. Only a step from Ava's own flat, it was extremely convenient, yet intended to remove any implications that they were living together. Their reunion was happy and intense.

On July 12, Frank made his British vaudeville debut at the London Palladium, with Ava in the front row center to give him support. The crowds of teenagers screamed and swooned as ecstatically as his American fans had done before his career started to wane. Ava was at once amused and shocked by their behavior. Frank's throat was completely healed, and his relationship with Ava in the London they both adored was more joyful than it had ever been. Frank sang surprisingly well and the reviews were ecstatic. The couple were invited to many parties, mingling with the aristocracy and royalty, including Princess Margaret.

In September 1950, Frankie and Ava returned to New York and went to nightclubs and fights, attracting great attention when they attended the Joe Louis-Ezzard Charles world heavyweight championship bout at Yankee Stadium.

Meanwhile, Nancy won a separate-maintenance suit in the Superior Court of Santa Monica. She was awarded the Holmby Hills house, a Cadillac, and the children's custody.

In October, Ava returned to Hollywood to appear in her next film for M-G-M, a version of Hammerstein and Kern's *Show Boat*. It was to be directed by George Sidney, who had handled Ava's first test.

"Everyone thought I was crazy to buy *Show Boat*," Sidney says. "And even crazier when they heard I was going to cast Ava as Julie, the tragic half-caste that Helen Morgan played originally. 'Ava?' they kept saying. 'She's nobody! Why cast her, of all people?' I can still remember Hedda and Louella calling me and begging me not to cast her. The studio top brass was dead against it. But I was determined. I *knew* she would be Julie.

"She was a 'second best' girl, she felt that, and she had a terrific inferiority complex. I knew that Helen Morgan had had the same sense of insecurity. And then, Ava was a Southern girl; she had a lilting accent that suited Julie perfectly. Ava went back to her North Carolina voice, and it was almost beautiful.

"We did the test with Ava mouthing to Lena Horne's voice in a couple of songs, and she was perfect. You never saw such patience and concentration! And she played the part so perfectly that in the scene in which she asks for some Scotch, the audience at every preview actually *applauded*! Those sons-of-bitches loved her!

"It's often been said that her voice wasn't good enough and that we only used it in the recording. That isn't true. We tried another singer, but she didn't have the heart-breaking quality of emotion we needed. I did everything, I grabbed that singer, tried to make her cry, kissed her, everything to make her come through with an emotion. It didn't work.

"Then Frankie put pressure on us, and so did she, that Ava do her own voice. I thought, 'Well, let's try it.' Unbelievably, it worked. She half-sang, half-spoke the lines and it was deeply moving. The whole unit clapped as she finished, and she started to cry. Unfortunately, though, at the last moment the studio made us replace her singing voice with that of a professional singer, Annette Warren. I was as upset as Ava was. And she was *upset*! But they did use her voice on the record."

Show Boat was a pleasant experience for Ava—she adored her co-star Kathryn Grayson—and it earned her great notices. Howard Keel vividly recalls making the picture with Ava. "It was a completely 'dry' studio, we were told. Anyone who was caught drinking risked the wrath of Louis B. Mayer and perhaps a suspension. So with the utmost caution Katie Grayson and I and Ava managed to smuggle tequilas into the dressing rooms, and we'd get happily sloshed at the end of a day's work. Next day we'd be back on the set, happy if hung over, and we'd emote as primly and properly as you could imagine. I don't think anybody knew the difference, or that we were far from being the clean-as-a-whistle saintly types Metro stars were supposed to be. If Mayer had ever found out he'd have had a heart attack."

By the time *Show Boat* was finished, Ava's original contract—beginning at $75 a week with six month options for seven years—had been renewed for another seven at $50,000 a year. The new contract was as rigid as its predecessor, calling for absolute rectitude, teetotalism while working, and immediate suspension if a role were refused.

Though Ava was earning good money now, M-G-M could make more money out of her by lending her to other studios for far more than her salary and not giving her a cent of the profits. For *One Touch of Venus*, Universal had paid $100,000 for five weeks' work, and since then her loan-out price had gone up to $120,000. Moreover, she had to live very carefully. Journalist Pete Martin reported in the *Saturday Evening Post* in 1951: "Even with her $50,000 a year she still had to live with comparative frugality. What with her manager-lawyer's fee and her agent's 10 percent cut, plus state and federal income taxes, about 71 percent of her pay is gone before she gets her hands on it. Her manager-lawyer only allows her $176 a week as expense money. Out of this she must pay her rent and maid's salary, as well as her clothing, food, lighting, auto upkeep, cleaning and drug bills. The rental for her apartment is $200 a month. That portion of her income which remains goes into savings."

At the end of each picture she made, Martin wrote, she had to hand over numerous tips to the craftsmen who made it. And she had to entertain lavishly to get the parts she wanted and the directors and cameramen she preferred.

Another problem was that she had to dress very expensively "off the sound stage," and yet she was not easy to fit with clothes. With her 36 inch hips, 36 inch bust, and 20 inch waist she could wear size 14, but she had an unusually long torso and her shoulders were narrow for her height, so practically everything had to be made for her. These were some of the problems Ava faced as she emerged to major international stardom after *Show Boat* in 1951.

Chapter 7

THE EARLY MONTHS OF 1951 were far from comfortable, for Frank was still married to Nancy, Ava was maddened by the delays in getting the divorce, and there was ferocious possessiveness on both sides. Despite the fact that the affair had continued for over a year, neither Ava nor Frank was secure in the relationship. The very similarity which had drawn them together made them quarrel constantly, placing them in direct conflict on a variety of subjects ranging from music to politics. Their reconciliations were as intense as their separations. They moved from Los Angeles, where Ava had shifted from the Nichols Canyon house (which she

gave to Bappie) to another in Pacific Palisades, to Palm
Springs and back again, their life a succession of lovers'
wranglings.

Pandora and the Flying Dutchman was held up from
release for months, the studio executives, including
Mayer, feeling that it was too literary to be tolerated by
the general public. But Ava was fascinated by the completed work, telling friends that she felt she had never
looked more beautiful than in the exquisite photography
of Jack Cardiff, though she also felt characteristically
that she had not given a particularly good performance.

During this period, Ava's personality had begun to
change. Now in her late twenties, she had coarsened and
become more harsh. The somewhat simple, sweet, and
tender quality of her earlier self was still often visible, but
the tough, extrovert slanginess of the other side of her
nature was emerging more strongly. Most found her
honesty crude but agreeably refreshing in a Hollywood
that operated on lies; a few were shocked by her acid
tongue and bearing. Certainly, her language had never
been more colorful than when M-G-M, in the spring of
1951, sent her a script by Borden Chase entitled *Lone
Star*, in which she was to play the role of Martha Craden,
a Texas newspaper woman of the 1840s.

From the outset, *Lone Star* was a doomed project.
First of all, no one could stand Borden Chase's script.
Mayer ordered rewrites, which did not work out, and
the director, Vincent Sherman, went into the film without
any enthusiasm at all. At first, Clark Gable, Ava's co-star,
threatened to take the whole thing off M-G-M's hands
and make it somewhere else as an independent production. This seemed agreeable, since he was "through" at
the box office at the time, and presented an increasing
photographic problem to the studio. He was suffering
from the first stages of Parkinson's disease, which made

his head shake uncontrollably. But Mayer, in view of Gable's fine record in the past, proceeded with the film.

Mayer wanted Ava to play the role of a girl reporter in love with Gable, and she was assigned to it on danger of suspension without salary if she refused.

Director Vincent Sherman says, "Since she was broke, she had no alternative but to accept. But she hated the part, and the idea of playing the one species of human being she despised above all others, a reporter, was abhorrent to her to the point of producing nausea. I was in wardrobe for discussions on Lionel Barrymore's clothes when I was told she wanted to see me. I hurried back to my office and found her sitting in my chair with her feet on the desk and her shoes kicked off. 'For Christ's sake, Sherman,' she said, 'haven't you got a drink around here?' 'Sorry,' I said cheerfully. 'Shall I send out for one?' 'No, don't bother,' she grinned dangerously. 'What in the name of Christ are you doing this for?' I shrugged. 'God knows,' I said. She relented slightly at that, then said, 'What am I doing playing a newspaper woman, a political newspaper woman? You know what I think of those jerks!' I liked her at once. She was frank and outspoken. When she saw I hated the script as much as she did and had gotten pressured into it, and when she saw I was 'up front' with her and on the level, she trusted me. We got on well."

Once she had accepted that she had no alternative but to do the film, Ava went ahead to make something of the ridiculous part. She and Gable vied with each other to be on the set first. Frank dropped by to give her moral support. In her love scenes with Gable, she gently tried to help conceal his convulsively shaking head. She was aware that much as he liked her, he had reached an age and a condition of health which made him resent her youth and vibrancy.

She liked the honest, reserved Sherman very much indeed. But when he started pressing books on psychology (including *Our Inner Conflicts* by Karen Horney) on her she shied away as though she'd been bitten by a hornet. Sherman says: "She yelled 'Oh Christ, Vince!' when I pushed a copy of Horney's book in her hand. 'I don't want to read any more books on neurosis. Artie Shaw fed me that crap and I'm so damned mixed up as a result I don't know what I'm doing.'"

Upset over her collapsing relationship with Sinatra, she often took her lunch alone while Sherman, Gable, and their great friend Spencer Tracy ate in the commissary. On the rare occasions she joined them, she loved Tracy's wit. When he heard that the prim studio boss, Dore Schary, cut a scene in which she walked joyfully down a street after spending a night with Gable, Tracy said, "Since Schary took over, nobody gets laid at M-G-M."

When the dull chore of making *Lone Star* was over, Ava told Frank she had to have a vacation in Mexico City. She had always adored Mexico: the art, the bullfights, the food, the booze—tequilas had become a special favorite of hers. Early in August, the couple started out on a flight to Mexico, where they had been offered accommodation by an old friend, an attractive blond society woman called Chiqui Gastel. But by the time they left for Mexico, Frank seemed to be on the verge of a nervous breakdown.

At Los Angeles International Airport, he looked pale, drawn, and ill with sleeplessness and strain. He refused to board the American Airlines Mexico Clipper until all the photographers were removed from the tarmac and the ramp. The photographers refused to leave, and became menacing when attempts were made to dislodge them: their jobs depended on getting a story. Finally, Ava made a dash for the plane, a copy of *Life* magazine over her head; Frank answered a plea from the airport staff to follow her 30 minutes later, and rushed into the plane scattering cameramen as he went.

Depressed and exhausted, the miserable couple sat holding hands until they reached El Paso for a 45 minute stopover. Once again, the press swooped, and Ava—in futile hope of keeping them quiet—said she was going to Mexico "for a vacation." They arrived in Mexico City on August 1, and were met by Chiqui. This time the press got a chance to talk to the couple, heard Frank's denial that the trip was to arrange a quick Mexican divorce from Nancy, heard him say that the journey was "purely for vacation purposes." The *Los Angeles Times* reported next day that "Frank's and Ava's attempt to slip quietly into Mexico by air last night turned into the most publicized romantic goings-on since Rita Hayworth and Prince Aly Khan."

On August 4, the pair left for Acapulco in a B-26 attack bomber, the private plane of the former baseball magnate Jorge Pasquel. They spent the first evening at a nightclub owned by Hedy Lamarr's husband, Ted Stauffer. Miss Lamarr, who was supposed to be the hostess at the club, pointedly ignored Ava, thus infuriating Frank, who threatened "reprisals." At one point in the evening, the couple walked onto the elaborate stone balcony of the club and necked passionately in the darkness, attracting a large audience. A nightclub patron said later, "They thought nobody could see them when they went out there to smooch in the dark. But they were wearing white clothes and it was better than any floor show."

On the night of August 8, Ava and Frank flew back to Los Angeles in Jorge Pasquel's bomber. Frank shook his fist at camera crews which tried to photograph him, then walked with Ava arm in arm out of the quarantine office. As they drove off in Frank's Cadillac convertible, a pho-

tographer, Bill Eccles, tried to shoot a picture of them
through the windshield. Frank swerved, perhaps accidentally knocking the photographer over, and screaming
at him, "Next time I'll kill you, you son-of-a-bitch!"

While Ava returned home, Frank flew almost at once
to Reno for a two week singing engagement at the Riverside Inn. Frank used his time in Reno to obtain a divorce
from Nancy. He told reporters, "I'm going to get it in the
simplest and quickest way. Nancy didn't want to come up
here for a divorce but she had no objection to my filing
for it." Asked why he became angered in Mexico he said,
"I got sore because I got pretty rough handling from a
couple of guys. They were the exceptions to the rule,
though, for the press has done a lot for me."

On August 19, he announced firmly, "Miss Gardner
and I will definitely be married."

Ava arrived that same day from a brief stopover in
Lake Tahoe. Asked about a fan magazine article over her
signature entitled "I'm Through with Romance," she said,
"Me? That must have been someone else you're thinking
of. I've never been through with romance at all!"

On August 22, Frank closed his engagement at the
Riverside Inn and flew with Ava to Las Vegas, where he
was booked into the Desert Inn. A week later, the couple
left for Lake Tahoe again, where they enjoyed a picnic on
Frank's new motor yacht. A sudden storm blew up, hit-
ting the yacht and drenching the picnic party. Frank
threw the anchor in the soft shale and the party jumped
over the side and waded, badly soaked, ashore. A sudden
violent gust of wind tilted the yacht and it capsized and
sank. It was the second accident to the yacht in a month:
on a previous excursion Frank had rammed it into a pier
and damaged the prow.

Frank and Ava planned to marry in Las Vegas as soon
as the Nevada divorce was final. On August 30, Ava was

in the headlines for getting a speeding ticket in Carson
City. Next month, the marriage was firmly announced,
but postponed again because the interlocutory decree was
still not available.

On September 17, the couple flew to Hollywood to
attend the premiere of *Show Boat* at the Egyptian Theater.
The theater was given an elaborate "Southern" look, with
black children jumping up and down to the sound of
banjos, bales of cotton piled high, and a reproduction of
the helm room of the great show boat *Cotton Blossom*
itself. Ava arrived with Frankie, looking marvelous in
an emerald green satin and black lace evening gown designed by Irene, a diamond necklace, and a Guilaroff
hairdo. The crowd screamed "Frankie!" and "Ava!" The
photographers swarmed around them, and they behaved
impeccably, smiling and bowing. A party at Romanoff's
was planned for later, but they drove off to Frank's house
instead: he had to report on the set of *Meet Danny
Wilson* at RKO the next morning.

The reviews of *Show Boat* were on the whole very
good. *Newsweek* wrote: "Ava does surprisingly well as
the mulatto Julie . . . visually and strictly on her own,
Miss Gardner makes a stunning Julie." *Time* said: "Ava
Gardner has no trouble looking her part as the sensuous
Julie."

On September 26, Frank and Ava were still impatiently
awaiting the divorce. That day, Ava, who had not been
sleeping well, collapsed with a severe virus infection and
extremely low blood pressure and was rushed to St.
John's Hospital in Santa Monica. She was forced to can-
cel a guest appearance with Bing Crosby on Bob Hope's
radio show and had to be replaced by Jane Russell. To
make matters worse, Frank could not be in constant attendance: he had to leave for New York, still with no
news of the divorce. Ava lay in the hospital for a month,

sparking comment that she might have had an abortion. Her doctor, William Weber Smith, simply said she was "tired and exhausted and had lost a lot of weight."

By October 19, she was still a little shaky, but able to get up and about and attend a party at Ciro's with the English actor Richard Greene. Inevitably, she was asked if she was "dating" Greene. She laughed: "The things people will say! I just happened to be in Richard's car!" But the rumors of a relationship obstinately persisted.

Frank was infuriated by stories of her affair with Greene and at his insistence Ava flew into New York on October 28. On November 2, the divorce from Nancy was finally granted, and Frank flew with Ava to Las Vegas for a four minute closed hearing before District Judge A. S. Henderson.

The way to the marriage was now completely clear. It was to have taken place at the Philadelphia home of Mr. and Mrs. Isaac Levy, great friends of Frank's for many years. But at the last moment the plans were changed: Frank decided to have it at the home of Lester Sacks, another friend, in the same city.

On November 3, Ava and Frank arrived in Philadelphia and filled out the marriage license application in the City Hall chambers of Judge Charles Klein. While Klein kept the reporters busy with an informal interview, the nervous couple fled out a rear exit and made their way down to the lobby in an elevator. Local law required a 72 hour wait before the marriage could be legal. After the blood tests and presentation of the documents covering their divorces, they lost their patience and drove around trying anxiously to find a judge who would marry them, any time, anywhere, without waiting the 72 hours. But this proved to be impossible.

The marriage took place on November 7. Like Ava's previous weddings, it was a quiet one: Bappie was there,

and Frank's parents, Frank's conductor Axel Stordahl
and his wife June, Frank's partner Ben Barton, and an
arranger, Dick Jones, who struck up Mendelssohn's Wedding March on the piano. As Ava started down the stairs
with Lester Sacks' brother Manny, who had been selected
to give her away, she leaned heavily on his arm, overcome with stage fright. He missed his footing and slid
with an undignified crash down several steps.

Recovering, the pair advanced steadily to the specially
prepared altar where Judge Sloane waited to perform the
ceremony. Ava looked beautiful in her Howard Greer
cocktail length dress of mauve-toned marquisette, stiffened
like brocade, with a strapless top of pink taffeta. She wore
a double strand of large pearls and small pearl and diamond earrings. The wedding bands worn by bride and
groom were narrow platinum circlets without ornament.

Axel Stordahl filmed the entire ceremony in color, and
the hosts entertained everyone with a lavish champagne
buffet. At 8:30 that evening, Ava put on her going-away
costume: a Christian Dior creation in dark brown, and a
sapphire mink stole which was Frank's wedding present
to her. She had given him a gold locket with St. Christopher and St. Francis medals on either side, and a picture
of her inside.

Determined to avoid another ghastly scene at the airport, Frank had chartered a twin-engine Beechcraft for
the honeymoon in Florida and Cuba. They left Philadelphia in such a rush that Ava forgot her trousseau
suitcase and remembered it only when she had climbed
abroad the plane. Shrugging, she said, "Let's fly to Miami
without it." On the plane, she changed into a casual outfit
she had brought with her in an overnight bag.

They arrived at dawn, and were driven by friends to
the Green Heron Hotel. By morning, the trousseau bag
sent on by the Levys had not arrived, and Ava had noth-

ing to wear for breakfast. So a maid bought some groceries for the newlyweds and Ava cooked the wedding breakfast—eggs in olive oil—in their suite.

That afternoon they wandered along a cold and windy beach, spotted by photographers who took some charming informal shots of them, dressed in an odd assortment of clothes, happily arm in arm.

Next day, the trousseau suitcase at last in hand, they flew to Havana. They spent two days in Cuba, sightseeing in a rented car and going to various nightspots. Then they flew to New York, where they visited with Axel and June Stordahl, Frank worked on a CBS television program, and they dined with the Sinatra parents at Hoboken, before flying to Los Angeles on November 15. The trip to the coast was rough and the plane was battered by severe headwinds. Ava was barely aware of the turbulence, but Frank was fretful and nervous all through the flight.

On December 7, 1951, the couple boarded a TWA Constellation jet bound for London, where Frank was booked to appear at the Royal Command Variety Performance. The Duke of Edinburgh threw a cocktail party for the various stars booked to appear, and Ava danced a samba with him.

No sooner had the Sinatras arrived home from the benefit than they discovered they were the victims of a burglary. On the night of December 9, someone had taken Frank's Christmas present to Ava—a diamond and emerald necklace—from its box on the dressing table, along with Frank's cameo cuff links and a platinum and sapphire ring. Ava was shocked into tears over the loss of the necklace: it was her favorite piece of jewelry.

Chapter 8

IN THE EARLY MONTHS OF 1952, Ava began work on a new project at 20th Century-Fox: a version of Hemingway's *The Snows of Kilimanjaro.* Hemingway's famous short story had first appeared in 1937. Darryl Zanuck, an aficionado of big game hunting in Africa, had wanted to make the film ever since before World War II. His problem had been to match Hemingway's stream-of-consciousness technique in telling the story of a mortally wounded big game hunter, who, in a camp at the base of Mount Kilimanjaro, recalls the story of his life.

After numerous studio attempts to solve the problems of the script, the experienced Casey Robinson, hitherto a leading writer at Warners, where he had written the screenplays for *Now, Voyager* and *Dark Victory*, was engaged for the task. Hemingway himself stayed out of the project, though he personally asked Zanuck to cast Ava in the role of Cynthia, the Twenties girl whom the big game hunter loved. Art director Lyle Wheeler prepared an African hunting camp on a Fox sound stage, backed by a 350 foot by 40 foot cyclorama canvas duplicating the African bush country around Mount Kilimanjaro, as well as sets of portions of the mountain itself, second unit shots of which were taken in Africa.

Gregory Peck was cast as Harry the big game hunter, Susan Hayward as Helen, his rich wife, and Hildegarde Neff as Harry's mistress, Countess Liz. At first, Anne Francis was seriously considered as Cynthia, but she lost the part because she failed to look sufficiently like Susan Hayward for the crucial scene in which Harry mistakes Miss Hayward for his lost Cynthia. So Ava was cast.

Casey Robinson says: "I had written the part of Cynthia, that lost Twenties girl, for Ava. I'd known her when she was young, a barefoot girl out of the tobacco fields. Now she came in to the Fox studio to see me and Henry King.

"All of the qualities I saw in her when she was young had developed in just the right way for Cynthia. How can I express the quality that she had? Think of the woman in Michael Arlen's *The Green Hat* . . . Iris March. Think of Willa Cather's Lost Lady. Think of Anna Karenina, even. A kind of doomed character, a character scheduled for misfortune. But one who had within her the capacity to stick out her chin and say 'Give it to me.' And to do it with a kind of pathetic laugh.

"She was just like those expatriate American women in Paris after World War I. I had been there, and I knew the very essence of that time. Her lover says to her, 'Do you paint?' 'No, I don't paint.' 'Do you sculpt?' 'No, I don't sculpt.' 'What do you do?' 'I only try to be happy.' That was Ava!

"I asked her if she wanted to play it. She said, 'Yes, very much, even though it's the third part, the third woman in the story.' I said, 'Miss Gardner, don't tell me you're a page counter. It's true you have less pages than the other women. But believe me, Cynthia is the female star. Because she's the very heart of the picture, she's the very heart of the story of the hero.'

"Ava said, 'I'm interested, very interested.' She paused and walked away. 'But I have a problem, a very great problem. My husband doesn't want me to play it. Frankie's against it.'

"She told me that Frank was so low, his career was so hopeless, that he needed her to go with him to New York, where he had a nightclub engagement. He insisted on it. It was quite a problem. So I sat down with Henry King, went over the schedule, and changed things around. We had to promise to shoot Ava's part in 10 days. On that promise, Sinatra said a reluctant okay.

"Now we were ready to go. Three days before we were due to start shooting she arrived at the studio. I took her to the wardrobe department and she accepted Anne Francis' clothes without a word. Here she is, about to be the star of Twentieth's most expensive production to date, and she has no temperament, no fire! Any other actress would have made us toss out Anne's clothes and make new ones for her. Not Ava.

"It *was* her part. She understood that line when Greg Peck, who meets her in a nightclub, said to her, 'Are you Charles' lady?' referring to her date, and she says, 'No, I'm my own lady.' She *was* her own lady. On the whole, she spoke the lines correctly. There was a small scene between her and Greg Peck in a cafe when she had to say something she didn't understand. She said, 'Casey, I don't

With Robert Mitchum in *My Forbidden Past*
(RKO RADIO PICTURES, INC.)

With Sheila Sim, Harold Warrender, and Nigel Patrick in
Pandora and the Flying Dutchman (M-G-M)

Right and opposite:
Ava Gardner in
*Pandora and the Flying
Dutchman* (M-G-M)

Above: With Kathryn Grayson, Agnes Moorehead, Joe E. Brown,
Regis Toomey, and Robert Sterling in *Show Boat* (M-G-M).
Below: With Clark Gable in a scene from *Lone Star*
(WIDE WORLD PHOTOS)

Ava and Frank Sinatra cut the wedding cake, November 7, 1951

With Gregory Peck in a scene from *The Snows of Kilimanjaro* (20TH CENTURY-FOX)

know what the hell I'm saying, but I'll say it anyhow.'
The language was too complicated for her, and the
thought processes contained in that language. She stum-
bled a little, she was nervous. But she got through it.

"And I think she was tense in the scene when she fell
down the stairs and aborted the baby. Originally, I had
written a line for her. 'Shall we have the baby, or get rid
of it?' I think it was fortunate that this went out.

"Came the ninth day of shooting. We had only one
more sequence to do. Frank kept calling her on the set
and making her life pretty darn miserable. I like Frank
now, but at the time I hated the little bastard because he
was making my girl unhappy. Now I understand him, he
was so beaten and insecure. Then came the last scene, the
scene on the battlefield in Spain when Ava is dying.
There was a problem: we had a great many extras, 400 or
500 in all, and to satisfy the 10 day agreement we'd have
to shoot into the night, which would have been horribly
expensive. We decided to go over the 10 days and break
the agreement. When King and I told Ava all hell broke
loose. She became hysterical. She called New York and
Frank was furious with her. God knows how we got
through that last day.

"But it was the right role for her, and it launched her
as a very great international star."

The part was uncannily right for Ava, not only as a
reflection of her own possessive personality—fiercely
loyal, generous, and devoted as well as coarse-grained,
unlucky, doomed, tragic—but in many ways as an astonishing prophecy of her future life in Spain. But it showed
a brilliant prescience on Hemingway's part to choose her
for the role, and it was an incredibly lucky break for
director Henry King, as he admits today, that Ava
played it. "No one else could have given it the sensitivity,
the bruised quality, that Ava imparted to it," he says.

She cut out drinking, late nights, and too much Frankie, and she disciplined herself rigorously for the part. King says: "She always could do this if she believed in a role—and she believed in Cynthia. Sometimes she'd come in grumbling in the morning—she hated to get up early and drive to the studio. But once she was actually on the floor she worked with a kind of desperate involvement and intensity that amazed me."

King—whose career stretched back to such silent classics as *Stella Dallas* and *Tol'able David*—and Ava became fast friends. She was genuinely sorry when the picture was over, and shocked when it ran into considerable flak from critics ("Meandering, pretentious, maudlin," *Newsweek* wrote). Most dismissed it as a travesty of Hemingway. Another problem was reported in *Variety*: several exhibitors' groups complained that since patrons could not pronounce the name Kilimanjaro, they were experiencing great difficulty in persuading anybody to see it. A round-robin letter exploring the matter was sent back to 20th Century-Fox's assistant sales chief W. G. Gehring, who wrote: "Our New York executives, including Mr. Skouras and Mr. Lichtman, have seen the picture in California. Both of these gentlemen are sure the title is just right. . . ." Casey Robinson wrote a long defense of the picture in *The New York Times*, pointing out that he had deliberately set the story in differing Hemingway locales to give it the correct flavor. Most critics—except the implacable Bosley Crowther—agreed that Ava Gardner was "surprisingly good" in the picture. Ruth Waterbury, writing for the *Los Angeles Examiner*, said: "The lovely Gardner, with the best part of the three women, takes over with warmth and tenderness." *Variety* wrote: "She makes the part of Cynthia a warm, appealing, alluring standout."

* * *

Early in May 1952, Ava visited Hawaii and told the local press she wanted "to go down in a U.S. Navy submarine in Pearl Harbor." The arrangements would have been strictly against naval regulations, but Lt. Comdr. Sweitzer of the submarine *Pickerel* decided to satisfy her demands. Once she was piped aboard he gave loud orders for the submarine to submerge. Bells clanged, the top was battened down, and there were loud gurgling noises. After a while, the submarine supposedly surfaced: actually all it had done was move unsubmerged a few hundred feet around the dock, but it was not until she got to the mainland that Ava discovered the truth.

Back in Hollywood on May 22, Ava planted her feet and hands in wet cement in a special ceremony in the forecourt of Grauman's Chinese Theater on Hollywood Boulevard.

On May 24, Ava was rushed to Cedars of Lebanon Hospital and underwent surgery, performed by Dr. Leon Krohn. She had just attended a performance of Frank's at the Cocoanut Grove. For days she had been feeling ill, not certain what was wrong with her, and terrified she might have cancer. Many people believed she had had another abortion, but the facts of her illness were never made public.

In June, Ava was handed a new script by M-G-M: *Ride, Vaquero*, a western set in the period just after the Civil War. Ava disliked the script, and when she arrived at the location she was desolate.

Making *Ride, Vaquero* proved to be an almost intolerable ordeal. Ava was flown with all other members of the company—except her co-star Robert Taylor who had his own private plane—to the unpleasant little town of Kanab in southern Utah. It was hot, stifling, and deadly, with wooden frame houses and only one seedy hotel, known as

Perry's, run by a man who had grown rich from previous westerns made there. When she arrived, Ava was horrified to find herself enveloped by a thin red dust which settled on clothes, face, and hair. The temperature was about 120 degrees, and her aluminum mobile dressing room, when shifted into a local canyon for some scenes, became uninhabitable. The first night she could not sleep at all: there was no air conditioning at Perry's and no pool to cool off in. She could hardly breathe; the dryness made her choke. She was afraid she would get a serious sinus and eye inflammation. She had to start the first morning with breakfast at 5 a.m. She told publicity man Jim Merrick as she entered the dining room, "I wish I were dead."

Her misery was so obvious that several members of the crew searched around for a house for her. They failed to find one. Finally, Perry, the owner of the hotel, was persuaded to lend her his own comparatively comfortable brick house just outside town. There, Ava was slightly more at ease. But she was shocked by the location site, with its flies, and blazing sunlight which shriveled the skin. The sweat ruined her makeup, making it trickle down her cheeks and into her lace collar. In desperation she called Frank and asked him to join her. He flew in at once for two weeks, doing his best to commiserate with her. But she could barely endure the experience even with him around. She disliked the director, the late John Farrow, because of his sadistic treatment of the horses. Farrow, husband of Maureen O'Sullivan, was a tough Australian who used to fly to Los Angeles on Saturdays, fly back the next morning with an armful of call girls to carouse and fornicate all through the Sabbath, then turn up on the set on Mondays with a hangover, cursing at everyone.

M-G-M threw Ava a bone on her return: a chance to

appear in a remake of the film *Red Dust*—opposite Clark Gable repeating his original role. *"Red Dust!"* she told a reporter. "Haven't I had enough of red dust in Utah?" But secretly she was extremely pleased at this fulfillment of an earlier dream.

The new picture was to be called *Mogambo*. The writer John Lee Mahin completely reconstructed *Red Dust*'s script. Originally, the setting had been the Malay Archipelago: the story had concerned Clark Gable's romantic entanglement with two contrasting women: a brassy chorus girl played by Jean Harlow and a lady of position played by Mary Astor. In the last scene, Gable chose to have an affair with Harlow. In the new version, Gable became an African big game hunter, who was more interested in the good woman (played by Grace Kelly) than in Honey Bear, the Harlow character cleverly reworked by Mahin to suit Ava's personality. *Mogambo* was Swahili dialect for "passion."

While the M-G-M production team left for preparations in Africa in September, Ava and Frank quarreled more and more frequently. Often the subjects of these arguments were Frank's children, and his frequent visits to Nancy's house to be with them. Ava could not shake off a feeling of terror that Frank might return to Nancy, simply in order to ensure his children a more secure upbringing. But in spite of all their problems, Frank seemed to improve technically in his singing and to have more self-assurance during those late summer and early fall months of 1952 than he had had in years. For all their quarreling, there was no question that the intense personal fulfillment the relationship brought him, the joys of a profound love, gave new meaning and depth to the lyrics he sang.

In September, however, a serious rift seemed to threaten the very foundation of the marriage. After Ava attended the New York premiere of *The Snows of Kilimanjaro*,

Frank picked her up and drove her to the Riviera night-club in Fort Lee, New Jersey, to attend his second performance. Ava was happy and energetic when she arrived, enjoying for once the eager stares of the crowd. But when she saw Marilyn Maxwell, a former girlfriend of Frank's, sitting out front she became extremely cool, and when Frank sang in Miss Maxwell's direction "All of Me" she flew into a rage, left the club after a violent series of expletives, and took the next available plane back to Hollywood, where she packed up her wedding ring and mailed it to the Riviera.

Frank played out a couple of depressed weeks at the Chase Hotel, St. Louis, before returning to Hollywood and reassuring Ava that Miss Maxwell was only a figure from the past and no longer meant anything to him. He drove her to Tijuana to attend the bullfights as a peace offering.

Shortly before leaving for Africa, Ava was involved in what was to become a notorious incident. On October 21, she gave a weekend house party at Frank's house, inviting Bappie, Ben Cole, Ava's business manager, and Lana Turner, another client of Cole's and an old friend of Ava's. One night all but Ava and Lana left the house to go to another party. Frank came home unexpectedly.

There were two versions of what happened next. The worst gossip was that Lana and Ava were in bed together. The other rumor was that Frank found them comparing his marital prowess with that of Artie Shaw, to whom Lana also had been married. Whichever the reason, Frank flew into a rage and demanded the two women leave the house. The quarrel became so violent that neighbors complained and called in Police Chief Gus Kettman to settle the matter.

My own view is that there was no truth to the lesbian

theory at all: it is much more likely that Ava and Lana were chuckling over the difference in sexual performance in their marriages to Artie Shaw. Since Frank was very jealous of Shaw, believing that Ava was still fascinated by him, the mere mention of Shaw's name would have been enough for him to cause a ruckus.

At any event, as a result of the incident Frank canceled his plans to travel to Africa with Ava. Then he reinstated them. In the meantime, Ava, who changed her phone number constantly, had it changed again, and Frank, unable to reach her, was forced to have Earl Wilson insert a plea for a reconciliation in his column. Ava answered the plea, called Frank, and traveled with him to appear at a rally ("Madly for Adlai") for the presidential candidate Adlai Stevenson in Las Vegas. Ava announced Frank on the stage with some show business schmaltz about "a wonderful, wonderful man," and they left at once for a visit to North Carolina, followed by a trip to New York and thence to Nairobi, Kenya, at the beginning of November.

For the trek into Kenya, Tanganyika, and Uganda, M-G-M had organized the greatest safari of modern times. Eight "white hunters" were engaged for the mobile film unit, which consisted of 175 whites and 350 natives. There were 13 dining tents, a traveling movie theater, an entertainment tent with pool tables, and lavishly upholstered tents better than many hotel rooms. There was even a fleet of planes, and of cars, including Landrovers and jeeps. One tent was fitted up as a hospital, with an X-ray unit, one as a sports area, with darts and table tennis, 16 for eating purposes, and one as a well-equipped kitchen. There was a traveling jail for the drunk and disorderly. Letters, food, and medical supplies were flown in daily from Nairobi to an 1800 yard airstrip hacked out of the jungles by John Ford's assistants. Film for the

Technicolor unit was stored by cameraman Robert Surtees in special refrigeration trucks, and was flown to Metro executives in Hollywood by daily airlift.

In a letter home, Clark Gable wrote: "For the first time in any film made in Africa, we have women portraying speaking roles although they jabber in their native tongue only. It wasn't difficult to get candidates: each morning one of our assistant directors would drive into the countryside in a truck. Within an hour he was back, usually with 20 or 30 women hanging onto the vehicle and even a few extra hiding under the seats. All were more than anxious to earn a few shillings by deserting their farm work (it is the women in Africa who perform all the menial tasks)."

Before she started work on the picture, Ava got barely a chance to meet the director, the legendary John Ford. Battered, bulky, with a gruff and harsh manner, Ford shocked Ava with his lack of deference for her star status and his apparent contempt for her as a woman. Known as a director of westerns, right-wing and rear-guard in his views, he was absolutely not Ava's type. During the first days of shooting she raged at his attitude toward her, his sheer hillbilly lack of grace. Finally, she turned away from him in a fury in the middle of a scene, exhausted by the heat, the flies, and Ford's intolerable rudeness. He beckoned her grimly to come away from the location site for a moment. She refused; he insisted. Then he said to her, "You're damned good. Just take it easy." From that moment on she understood that his manner was simply a defense mechanism, that he really admired her enormously. Later, he told me, "She was a real trouper. She was unhappy over Sinatra, but she worked her ass off just the same. I loved her."

In later years, Ava always said she hated Africa. But at the outset she enjoyed the challenge of the unusual location, the excellence of her native servants and bearers, and the opulence of her traveling tent, far more elaborate than any dressing room in Hollywood.

The first day's shooting was at Thika, Kenya; it was largely ruined by a large baboon which kept popping up in camera range to watch a love scene between Ava and Gable. There followed a harrowing journey by truck to Tanganyika, where several weeks of shooting took place, with cast and crew housed in a tent colony. Hundreds of tribesmen, many of them traditional enemies, were flown in by a massive airlift, including 68 members of the Wagenia tribe of the Belgian Congo, hired by producer Sam Zimbalist because they could paddle down river rapids for one scene. Shooting at the Kagera Rapids almost came to a halt when the Wagenia chiefs decided that the area was not propitious: their tribal gods were not present on the river. Zimbalist immediately chartered a plane and had it fly to Léopoldville to collect, at great expense, three tribal chieftains, who arrived and gave their blessings to the hazardous sequence.

Troubled by the constant prowling and growling of lions outside her tent, Ava hung a lantern which effectively drove them off. She was fascinated by Frank ("Bunny") Allen, the great white hunter who earned his living by arranging for movie safaris, but she refused pointblank to kill any wild animals, unlike Clark Gable who frequently accompanied Allen to the slaughter.

The expedition moved on past the Kagera River. The company encountered violent rainstorms and floods. "Ava loved the hardship," cameraman Robert Surtees says. "She even reveled in her canvas bathtub. She had a boy assigned to her, who would heat water over a fire while she was out shooting. When she came back her hot water was prepared to the exact temperature she wanted with a special thermometer, and her clothes were laid out exactly. Some of the British officials working on the picture sent a letter of complaint to the M-G-M people in Nairobi complaining that Ava was disporting herself naked before the natives in her bathtub. I'll never forget Ava's reaction when she got word of this. She roared with laughter, and immediately flung her clothes off, running bare-assed through the camp to the shower in front of everyone."

There were many days of drenching rain; Ava waited in her tent with the rest of the unit for the sun to break through. The shooting of some sequences in Kenya had to be done under armed guard. M-G-M had its own specially appointed police force which kept the cast from being attacked by Mau Mau terrorists.

One difficult scene showed a huge rhinoceros attacking a car in which Gardner and Gable were riding through the jungle. To shoot the scene Bunny Allen was at the wheel of the camera car following just behind them. As the sequence was being shot by Surtees, two other rhinos came up and all three charged the camera truck, throwing it out of control and sending it hurtling 100 yards along the dirt road while Surtees and Allen hung on grimly. Allen managed to grab his rifle and kill two of the animals; the third one ran off into the undergrowth.

"As a rule," Robert Surtees says, "the danger was never from animals. It was from automobiles. We ran over a couple of kids, and a visiting Hindu group of fanatics upset one of the cars. John Hancock, the 26-year-old assistant director, was killed when his jeep overturned and crashed. But the wild animals behaved perfectly and the toughest thing in the world was to make them look menacing.

"Ava provided menaces of her own—to American-British relations. John Ford thought it would be funny to have the governor and his lady meet Ava. He tried to put her on by saying, 'Ava, why don't you tell the governor what you see in this 120 pound runt you're married to.' And she said, 'Well, there's only 10 pounds of Frank but there's 110 pounds of cock!' Ford went green and said, 'I'll never talk to that girl again,' but the governor loved it. He and his wife fell over laughing."

Ava and Frank celebrated their first wedding anniversary in Africa. "It was quite an occasion for me," Ava said later. "I had been married twice but never for a whole year." Frank gave her a beautiful anniversary ring. A few days later, Robert Surtees said to Ava, "How could he afford that? The poor guy's broke, isn't he?" She turned to him and snarled, "You know what that son-of-a-bitch did? I got the bill for the ring!"

Frank's stay in Africa was not a happy one. He was restless and bored. He was aggravated by the heat and the difficult locations, and he and Ava quarreled constantly. Moreover, he was fretting because he wanted to play the important role of Maggio, a put-upon buck private, in the film of James Jones' best-selling novel, *From Here to Eternity*. Before she left Hollywood, Ava had begged Harry Cohn, boss of Columbia Pictures, to give Frank the part. When a cable arrived from Hollywood offering him the chance of a screen test, he immediately boarded the next plane, flying back to Africa three weeks later with the test completed.

He won the role. But in the meantime, Ava underwent a crisis. Pregnant for some time, she began suffering from the heat which in the early days of shooting had not seriously affected her. She flew to London for what she later called a "miscarriage." She told reporter Joe Hyams in 1956: "I was hospitalized secretly in a nursing home for four days with what was called in the newspapers 'a severe case of anemia.' All of my life I had wanted a baby and the news that I lost him (I'm sure that it was a boy) was the cruelest blow I had ever received. Even though my marriage to Frank was getting shakier every day I didn't care. I wanted a baby by him."

Robert Surtees says: "That isn't the way it was at all. Ava hated Frank so intensely by this stage she couldn't stand the idea of having his baby. She went to London to have an abortion. I know, because my wife went to London to be at her side at all times through the operation and afterward, and to bring her back on the plane. She told my wife, 'I hated Frankie so much. I wanted that baby to go unborn.'"

Back in Africa, sick and guilty and miserable, Ava no longer enjoyed the shooting, and it was an agony struggling through various comedy scenes. But Frank's return just before Christmas turned out to be unexpectedly bearable. After he won the role of Maggio, his desperation, bad nerves, and sense of hopelessness changed to an air of quiet triumph. He delighted Ava on arrival by pulling out of his suitcases boxes of noodles and cans of spaghetti in sauce, and she felt better than she had in weeks as they pitched in on the range of their mobile kitchen and prepared a giant Italian feast. Grace Kelly, Clark Gable, John Ford, Robert Surtees, and the rest of the unit had a wonderful time, but, Ava said later, "A generator burned out and we were all plunged in darkness. Everyone blamed it on the time I had taken to cook the spaghetti!"

Ava's Christmas Eve birthday celebration and Christmas Day were major events, bringing Frank and Ava closer than they had been in months. She told Joe Hyams: "Frank was charming as he usually is when he has an audience. He sang Christmas songs, and the natives, draped in blankets, sang carols in French, and John Ford read ' 'Twas the Night before Christmas.' After the songs everyone went off to bed and Frank and I sat in front of our tent and opened our presents.

"He had fixed a tiny tree right in front of our tent and had decorated it beautifully—even to little colored lights. His presents to me were a beautiful mink stole and a diamond ring.

"Frank's best present to me, though, was a shower he had rigged up for me. It consisted of a pump that took the river water through a pipe and then down over my head. He charmed the unit carpenter into building a little wooden hut around his gadget, and every evening at sundown Frank would pump water up from the river for me.

"We had spats almost daily including one or two that weren't our fault. One night just after Frank had arrived back in Africa we went to celebrate at a party in one of Nairobi's best nightspots. Frankie and I were holding hands and talking when a drunk lurched across the room and put his hand heavily on my shoulder.

" 'I want to dance with you,' he said thickly. I told him I was sorry, I wasn't dancing this one. The man left but as soon as the music started up he was back again. 'Hey, Sinatra,' he said, 'I want to dance with your wife.'

"Frank kept his temper. 'She's already told you she's not dancing,' he said and turned his back on the man.

"About a half hour later Frank asked me to dance and the drunk reappeared. 'Hey Sinatra,' he said, 'I thought she wasn't dancing.'

"Frankie turned around and said, 'Mr. Sinatra, if you don't mind.' Without another word the drunk swung at Frankie who ducked and hit him back. Within a few seconds they were mixing it up and Frank was giving better than he got.

"Friends broke them apart and the manager came over and asked us to leave. He assumed, automatically, that because we were film people we were at fault. The press, of course, also gave us the worst of it."

The shooting of *Mogambo* completed, Ava flew with the Surteeses to Rome while Frank returned to Hollywood to prepare for *From Here to Eternity*. "As soon as we got to the Eternal City," Surtees says, "Ava told me as a joke that she wanted to see every whorehouse in the city in one night. I had worked there on *Quo Vadis* for over a year so I knew where all the brothels were. She knew I'd know. Grace Kelly was staying, like Ava, at the Hotel Excelsior. I went over and picked the two of them up, as that cool, dignified Grace also wanted to go on the tour. Well, at one dive we got to a guy who became attracted to Grace and got in the back of the car to neck with her as we drove along. Ava laughed till I thought she'd burst. We'd go to one place after another; Ava loved to talk to the girls and exchange raw and ribald jokes with them, and it wasn't until three in the morning, after we'd tied on quite a few, that we got back to the Excelsior. I bundled the girls off to bed—God knows what my wife would have thought of all this—and next day at two, Ava called me and laughed. 'You no good son-of-a-bitch!' she yelled. 'What the fuck did you mean by keeping us up to 3 a.m.?'"

From Rome, Ava flew to London to complete interior scenes for *Mogambo* and start her next picture, *Knights of the Round Table*, for Pandro S. Berman, who had also produced *The Bribe*. In one scene for *Mogambo* shot at the M-G-M London studios she had to lie still while a well-trained snake slithered over her bed; she played it without a murmur.

Knights of the Round Table was a pet project of Berman's, who had wanted to make a follow-up to his very successful film of Sir Walter Scott's *Ivanhoe*, starring Robert Taylor and Elizabeth Taylor. He had always liked the story of King Arthur and his knights. Berman felt it unlikely that Elizabeth Taylor would want to make another film so similar to the first, but he insisted upon Robert Taylor's playing Lancelot, as he looked good in period clothes. He decided to cast Ava as Guinevere. "We weren't trying for art," Berman says, "we were trying for a down-to-earth mass entertainment picture. It seemed more appropriate to use a beautiful woman than use someone who was a better actress but mightn't have the mass sex appeal Ava had by that time. And she didn't have such a huge part that it would have been beyond her."

The decision was made to shoot the picture in England using the castle built for *Ivanhoe* at the Boreham Wood backlot of M-G-M's British studios. The windswept expanse of Dartmoor, in the west of England, was used for another location. The major difficulty in making the picture was that the English weather was even viler than usual.

Ava was depressed by the cold, drizzly conditions of shooting in the west of England. She was shocked when producer Berman and director Richard Thorpe told her the only sunlight in that area was during the hour or so after dawn. This meant that she and everyone else had to rise at first daylight and drive from their temporary homes in nearby villages to shoot while there was still some watery early sun; after that the fog and mist and rain would come in. This was tormenting for Ava, who was not only bored by the village life, but was unable to sleep. She had to rise at 5 a.m. to get into complicated royal costumes and heavy makeup.

An extras' strike forced Berman and Thorpe to make a particular battle scene in Ireland. The extras refused to wear the difficult and heavy armor needed unless they were paid a special bonus. Berman and M-G-M were quite prepared to pay this amount, but the British Association of Motion Picture Producers refused to give its consent to the extras being used at all. Berman was forced to cast actors as extras in the indoor scenes shot at the studio; for the battle scene he had to approach the Eire government to allow him to use their soldiers. The Guinness heiress loaned her great estate a little way out of Dublin, and Ava and the rest stayed at local hotels.

Under the direction of the second unit man Yakima Canutt, 100 trained stunt riders were brought from Hollywood to form the nucleus about which the battle armies of King Arthur could be built. Four times the usual number of riders were needed for the CinemaScope scenes. An army of accountants, transportation experts, and caterers, as well as 1000 trained cavalry and infantry, was assembled. It was difficult to jam the cast and crew into Dublin at the height of the tourist season, for Catholic groups from the United States were booked en masse. The caterers had to provide a hot lunch for a total of 3000 people every day. One day's M-G-M shopping list shows 975 pork chops, 300 pounds of potatoes, 340 loaves of bread, 150 large cans of peas, 1500 apples and pears, 400 gallons of coffee and tea, and 2000 cakes and buns.

Unemployed people poured in looking for work. Rain drenched down, and during a charge scene a number of riders fell as their horses slithered in the mud.

Reflecting her disinterest in the role, Ava played Guinevere with a wooden graciousness, looking tired and distinctly uncomfortable in many scenes. She got very bad reviews for her performance and agreed with them. "What was I doing in that costume epic, for heaven's sake?" she said to a reporter from *Photoplay*. Frank's visits to her on the dreary locations were accompanied by quarrels, and she realized finally that she had tired of him, finding him no longer charming but overbearing and impossible to live with. The only consolation was that her

income was now very large indeed: a reconstructed contract called for $17,300 a week for 50 weeks a year, and
only two pictures to be made in that period. But even that
consolation, like everything else in Ava's life, contained
an irony. M-G-M could now charge $200,000 to any
other studio that had need of her services.

Chapter 9

So it had become obvious that the Sinatras' marriage wasn't going to continue for very long. Their separate picture-making commitments, their constant traveling, the fact that Ava would start out for the studio at 6:30 a.m. when Frank was trying to sleep after a late night concert, and the endless pressures, tensions, and insecurities of their professional lives—all of these factors conspired to tear them apart. Worse, their similarities were nagging reminders: each could see his own faults in the other. Only their humor, dry and laconic, and their enormous generosities in every direction were plus factors.

A major problem was Frank's sudden shift from failure

to success. When he had been down, beaten, exhausted, he had been deeply neurotic and difficult, but at least he had clung to Ava, had depended on her, and he had enjoyed, on and off, this dependence. But now that his record sales were picking up, he began to assume a dominant role in the relationship. He became proud, fierce, competitive, full of machismo. He saw more and more of his circle of cronies. He needed her less and less, and she knew it.

Nineteen fifty-three was another year of constant moving about, of quarrels and reconciliations. Ava flew to Madrid in April, followed by a trip to Rome with Frank in May.

On May 16, Ava was due to appear with Frank at a concert hall in Naples, but at the last moment she became terrified of the crowd and hid in her hotel. When Frank went on stage alone at the matinee, he was greeted with whistles, shouts, and boos, and calls of "Ava! Ava!" That night the boos started again and he stalked, pale-faced, off the stage, after one song. Under persuasion from the chief of police of Naples, Fausto Salvatore, who feared a riot, Frank returned and told the audience, "Ma vedere che passa" ("Take it easy"). Meanwhile, annoyed by word of what had happened at the matinee, and afraid of being mobbed at her hotel, Ava fled to Milan.

In late fall, after almost nonstop moving about, she was in Hollywood for the first time in a year, to attend the opening of *Mogambo*. The reviews and the public reception were exciting, many critics commenting especially on Ava's sense of comedy timing, the sensibility she displayed in scenes with the animals, and the warmth with which she responded to John Ford's direction. She was, for once, not cynical about the reviews, reluctantly agreeing that she was "not bad" in the picture. Meantime, Frank had appeared in *From Here to Eternity*, startling everyone at the studio—and later the critics—with an impassioned, brilliant, intense performance which later won him an Oscar.

A serious rift took place in October when Ava and Frank both arrived in New York simultaneously, Frank staying at the Waldorf Towers and Ava at the Hampshire House. Ava was heard to complain to friends that Frank had not met her at the plane; Hedda Hopper called Frank from Hollywood, imperiously demanding an explanation. "I can't understand it," Frank said. "I drove to New York from Atlantic City, where I got off work at 4:30 a.m., and checked into my hotel, slept until 2 p.m., picked up a newspaper, and saw a picture of Ava at the airport. That's the first inkling that I had she was in town. We had no trouble. I don't know what she has in mind. It's a crying shame because everything was going so right between us." Then Hedda called Ava, wrung from her an admission that there had been a fight by transatlantic telephone, and snapped, "Well, if you two brats make up and come home, I'll give you a welcome home party."

Soon after, Ava was back in Palm Springs, keeping her fingers crossed that she would not have to suffer the ordeal of making *Green Fire*, a film about emeralds, in the steaming jungles of Colombia, South America. Luckily, the female lead went to the much tougher Grace Kelly. Ava was more interested in making a film called *St. Louis Woman* with Frank. But nothing came of this. For a time she was idle, recovering slowly and painfully from the long sojourn abroad. She became restive, angered particularly when her name was coupled on radio and television with big game hunter Bunny Allen, who had come to Hollywood on a publicity jaunt.

In late October, she called Hedda and Louella and told them that nothing could be done to patch things up. Frank's refusal to stay in England until she finished

Knights of the Round Table, she said, had caused a final rift. It seemed easier than saying that their very marital proximity was a torment by now.

Newspaper reports were a monotonous account of Frank's arriving at airports, brushing aside reporters with a scowl, and refusing to discuss the marital rift. Ava stayed at her Palm Springs house in seclusion, depressed by the bad publicity. It was during this dismal fall that she evidently decided to leave America as a home base for good. Everything seemed sterile and hopeless to her.

On October 31, in Carson City, Nevada, Frank finally admitted to the press that the marriage was all washed up. Ill and exhausted by the breakdown of the relationship, he spent some time in Mount Sinai Hospital in New York for a series of tests and a complete rest. Ava was worried about him, but refused to fly to his bedside.

She was very busy reading a script sent her by United Artists for a film tailor-made to her specific requirements: *The Barefoot Contessa*. It was written, and to be directed, by Joseph L. Mankiewicz, whose *All About Eve* had been a major comedy success. Mankiewicz had devised the entire script for her, basing the character she played on Rita Hayworth, and the character of the millionaire who loved her on Howard Hughes.

As usual, Metro was refusing to release her, and as usual she was furious. It was months before arrangements were completed for her to be borrowed for the picture, which was to start shooting in Rome. The moment she heard that she was to play the part she flew to Italy. Mankiewicz met her in Rome and helped her check into the Grand Hotel. She disliked the hotel at once and began to look for a house. Finally, she gave up and settled on an apartment in the Corso d'Italia, according to publicist David Hanna an ugly, sprawling, and noisy place filled with the sounds of street traffic. She organized her first press conference with a great deal of theatrical flair in the Grand Hotel ballroom, insisting upon subdued lighting and a full orchestra to play mood music. The press capitulated at once to her charm, and she became overnight the toast of Rome.

She insisted upon flying back to her home in Madrid for the Christmas holidays, returning—to everyone's astonishment—with Frank, whom she had met in Madrid. The company threw a lavish New Year's Eve party; Ava hated it, and to make things even worse came down with an attack of German measles.

In Madrid, Ava's friend Betty Wallers speaks of a typical incident: "We were at a bullfight. Curro Girón plunged his sword into the bull's heart and Ava leaped to her feet in homage. She flung a gold cross, set with turquoises and other precious stones, at his feet. Then she turned to me with a groan and said, 'That cross was a special present from Frank. I must get it back.' Terrified that Frank would find out the cross was missing, she arranged a dinner party for Girón. And she made him give the cross back."

The Barefoot Contessa, like *Singapore* and *The Killers*, concerned a woman seen through a haze of memory, an idealized figure, abstract and divorced from time. This time it was the story of Maria Vargas, a Spanish girl who started her career in local nightclubs, became a famous movie star who loved to go barefoot, and whose life was ended by her impotent Italian husband.

Mankiewicz' writing and direction of the picture came from his inside knowledge of Hollywood and international society; his lines were bitterly precise and harsh. Ava's playing left nobody in doubt that she could have captivated a long list of men, and she was dressed in clothes which accented her best features strikingly. Her playing was skillful, but she could not quite overcome the handicap of not being Spanish.

She worked with her usual desperate intensity on the part. Edmond O'Brien, who played a press agent, remembers how she plunged into an icy Mediterranean in midwinter for one scene and emerged looking as warm as though it were high summer. The toughest sequence was a dance, a ferocious display of a man-woman relationship worked out as a flamenco duet. "We practiced it every night for three weeks," she said later. "And those studio floors were cold." The scene was rehearsed at Cinecitta, and shot in Tivoli, outside of Rome, in an olive tree grove. It took many hours; Ava's bare feet were painfully torn. At the end, as she sank into her star's chair, the crew and 100 gypsies hired for the scene applauded her spontaneously.

Mankiewicz directed the film at tremendous speed: he shot 15 setups a day, a record at Cinecitta. He achieved this grueling pace, according to *Variety*, by arranging for his production manager, F. E. Johnston, to fine all latecomers to the set, the proceeds to be turned over to union welfare funds. At Portofino and San Remo, between January and March of 1954, the bitterly cold location shooting continued. Rain and icy winds constantly interrupted shooting, and her co-star Rossano Brazzi infuriated Ava with his constant complaints.

Her chief consolation during her ordeal was a new and passionate lover, Luis Miguel Dominguin, the handsomest and most distinguished bullfighter in Spain. They had met through mutual friends, the Sicres, and Ava had fallen deeply in love with him. He was absolutely Ava's type: tall, lean, hard, with broad shoulders and narrow hips and a very dark skin. He was a millionaire, the scion of a great family, refined and brilliant; he numbered Picasso and Stravinsky among his personal friends, and he mingled in the highest circles of international society. Ava adored his wit, his intellect, his physical beauty, and his consideration for her needs. Though she resolutely refused to live with him, she saw him constantly, causing ferocious gossip in Spanish Catholic society.

Her quarrels with Frank in Rome were as widely publicized as ever, and everyone was enormously relieved when he flew back to Hollywood early in January. Meanwhile, Dominguin and Bappie arrived at the Corso hotel.

With Dominguin and Bappie at her side, Ava felt she had all of the moral support she needed to work at her best. She dedicated herself to giving the performance of her career.

The only drawback was that Humphrey Bogart, who played one of her lovers in the film, hated her. He felt she was far too self-important and "royal," and he constantly tried to unsettle her in key scenes. It was all Mankiewicz could do to prevent a pitched battle between his stars on the set; at Portofino the tension became unbearable between the two players.

Fortunately, Bogart was not present on the location at San Remo. It was here that a story appeared which made world headlines. During the shooting of the picture, United Press reported that Ava and several friends had gone sightseeing on a small boat off the coast near San Remo, a storm blew up and the party lost control of the vessel. "A large yacht," UPI reported, "owned by the Rizzoli Film Company was ordered out to search for the craft. It found the sailboat after a four hour quest and towed it to safety. Friends of the actress said she escaped injury. They added, however, that she was very scared and her nerves were extremely strained." Reading this story in her suite at the Hotel Savoy, Ava doubled over laughing. The whole story was the invention of studio press agent David Hanna.

The film was completed in the last week of March 1954 in Rome. Rizzoli-Hagalag Films and *Figaro* gave a farewell party for the cast at the Open Gate Club. Nearly everyone went on to the airport to see Ava off to Madrid the following day. The Bogarts left for London and the Mankiewiczes proceeded to the Cannes Film Festival.

That March, Frank Sinatra won the Oscar for *From Here to Eternity*. Ava had been nominated for *Mogambo* but didn't feel she should win, and was in many ways relieved that she lost. Despite their separation, she sent a telegram of warmest congratulations to Frank on his success, and told everyone that she was overjoyed at his achievement.

A month later, *The Barefoot Contessa* finally in the can, Ava was in Madrid suffering from acute agony and discomfort from an attack of gallstones. In May, Ava was still in the hospital, suffering from pains so severe they made her weep uncontrollaby, and even fall to the floor screaming. Her doctor did his best to keep her quiet with sedatives, and Dominguin was constantly at her bedside, wearing himself out so completely while he was recovering from a goring by a bull that friends were worried about his health. When they urged him to have treatment, he simply checked into a hospital room near Ava's.

One evening, looking thin and ashen, he left the hospital and visited his close friend Ernest Hemingway, who was ill at the Palace Hotel, and told him it would be wonderful if Hemingway could go and see Ava. Hemingway, who had always admired Ava and had liked *The Killers* better than any other versions of his work, happily agreed. Rather unsteadily, accompanied by his wife Mary, his friend A. E. Hotchner, and Dominguin, he made his way to her room, where she was surrounded by a flock of nuns. Hotchner remembers that she was talking to a studio executive long distance, angrily refusing the role of the torch singer Ruth Etting in M-G-M's planned version of her life, *Love Me or Leave Me* ("What in Christ are you trying to do to me . . . I stand there mouthing words like a great goldfish while you're piping in some goddamn dubbed voice!").

A ridiculous press story of the time had Ava extending a delicate hand from the bedsheets and saying, "I've been waiting to meet you for years. You're my favorite author." Hotchner's version is more convincing: he quotes her as saying, "I love this damn hospital so much I almost don't want to pass this goddamn stone. Sit here on the bed, Papa, and talk to me. I'm absolutely floored you could come."

It was the beginning of a firm, absolutely platonic friendship in the years to come. Hemingway even collected one of the gallstones as a souvenir. By May 26, the relationship with Dominguin was three months old, and as intense as ever. Hemingway smiled on it, recognizing that the lovers had a great deal in common despite the rather comic language barrier: Dominguin spoke little or no English, Ava was still mastering Spanish, and some of his passionate protestations required an interpreter.

It was this affair which confirmed Ava in her conviction that she must end the marriage with Frank once and for all. She flew to London and Los Angeles on May 26, walked past reporters wearing a chilly smile and a charcoal suit, and moved on to Lake Tahoe to take up residence for a Nevada divorce. "Since all three of her husbands were in Las Vegas performing," a friend says, "she certainly didn't want to be caught dead in that city."

In the meantime, Ava had infuriated the studio by her refusal to play Ruth Etting, and she was put on suspension. She laughed the complaints off, and drove off, very fast, to Lake Tahoe. Hedda Hopper managed to corner her in a restaurant just before she left and heard some generalities about her desire to live in Spain, her lack of serious interest in Dominguin ("But isn't he handsome?"), and the end of her marriage ("Sinatra and I aren't going to be together again—ever").

In June, Ava was in a rented lodge in Lake Tahoe, waiting for the divorce from Frank to go through, and making side trips to Reno for gambling. Dominguin flew in on July 7 to join her, holding her hand tight as she lost money at the roulette tables. They toured Reno together taking in practically every club in town, and at night one reporter coolly observed, "She took lessons from him in Spanish."

The only serious problem in the relationship was that it took place on Howard Hughes' territory. Ava later told her publicist David Hanna that Hughes made life uncomfortable for Dominguin during his stay, and that Dominguin became restless and decided to return home.

But when Dominguin returned to Spain on July 15, Ava again took up with Howard Hughes, and several reporters noticed them going to nightspots together, holding hands and kissing. On July 27, she began preparing for a trip to South America to promote *The Barefoot Contessa*. Crowds greeted her ecstatically in Peru and Chile, and in Rio a huge mob was at the airport to cheer her as she stepped—a nice theatrical touch—barefoot from the plane. She drove off with 16 suitcases, accompanied by M-G-M representatives, to the Hotel Gloria, where she was under special armed police guard day and night.

That night, she flung a hectic party, so disturbing to the other guests that the manager asked her to leave the hotel at 4:45 a.m. Members of the staff descended on her suite with a bill for a smashed table, splintered glasses, smashed pictures, and wine stains on the walls. Ava screamed abuse at them, and announced, according to the wire services, "I will not stay another day in this country." But the United Artists people and friends managed to calm her and whisk her off to the Copacabana Palace, where she refused to see anyone.

Back in New York, Ava denied she had caused an incident, saying that the Gloria Hotel episode was "a complete lie provoked by anti-American feelings." "I didn't throw a glass at the wall as they said," she laughed. "I threw one on the floor. I'll never go to Brazil again!"

Chapter 10

SOON AFTER AVA'S RETURN from South America, she was faced with a major problem: *Confidential Magazine* published a story stating that, while still married to Frank, she was having an adulterous affair with Sammy Davis, Jr. The same article accused her of being involved with a number of "bronze boyfriends." The writer claimed her affair with Davis had been assumed because she had left her suite at the Drake Hotel in New York shortly after the South American trip and driven to the Apollo Theater to see Davis' late night show and join him for a comic number on the stage. Later, they were seen together at the Shalimar, a Seventh Avenue nightspot; and *Confidential* inaccurately had Ava slipping into Davis' suite at the Hotel Warwick for several assignations. She had long been a friend of Davis—since 1952 in fact—but the absurd article, riddled with inaccuracies, exasperated her.

The premiere of *The Barefoot Contessa* at the Capitol Theater in New York was a huge success, and Ava made a strong impression both in person and on the screen.

In New York after the opening, Ava agreed to pose for a series of portrait studies by photographer Philippe Halsman. She agreed on condition that a string quartet play mood music. The musicians arrived at the photographer's and began rehearsing so vigorously nobody heard when she pressed the doorbell. She went back to her hotel. Later, she returned and this time was heard. She sang and danced to Spanish music for three hours, then sat on the floor and said, "Don't you boys know any Beethoven?"

Back in Palm Springs, Ava rested comfortably at a modest house Howard Hughes had bought her: near the airport, so that he would be able to fly in his private plane whenever he felt like it. He even had special bodyguard-spies watching her at all times: she frequently asked the men in for a drink.

Hughes still wanted to marry her, seizing on the collapse of her marriage to Frank to pursue the matter again, but Ava persistently refused. Despite the convenience of this extraordinary continuing affair, with a plane always ready to take her to Mexico when she felt like it, she remained bored by the relationship. When Hughes flew into Palm Springs with $250,000 in cash seeking her to play a role in a particular film, she simply refused pointblank. But his devotion remained as deep as ever.

It was during this period at Palm Springs, with Hughes' spies constantly in attendance and his visits with expensive gifts more frequent than ever, that Ava met the ambitious and intense young journalist Joe Hyams, sent to

interview her by the *New York Herald-Tribune*. He was
thin, dark, strikingly handsome, as much Ava's type as
Sinatra, Dominguin, Mario Cabre, Walter Chiari, or any
other of the dark, hard, and lean lovers.

Today, Hyams is married to the German-born actress
Elke Sommer, and lives in an opulent house in Beverly
Hills, decorated with massive leather sofas, chunky
lamps, and a vivid collection of Elke's own paintings. He
tells the story of the pass Ava made at him. "I drove to
Palm Springs from Los Angeles," he says. "Though it was
attractively furnished, I thought her house was more like
that of a well-paid secretary than that of a movie star.
Ava greeted me in unaffected Spanish clothes, again quite
un-starry in style. She drank hard liquor and talked
pleasantly about a number of subjects. I had a concealed
tape recorder, the wires attached to a watch-sized recording device on my wrist. I told her about the recorder, and
she did not mind this so long as she could see the instrument. I also had a notebook in one pocket with a pencil
so that I could scratch descriptive data later on.

"As we talked on, the day started to fade. She suddenly
decided she wanted to buy some tequila. Since the only
place which sold it in Palm Springs—a small club—was
closed, she said on an impulse that we should drive to
Mexicali, across the Mexican border, to buy some. Ava
did not have a car; the only one in the house belonged to
her maid Mearene. I drove to Mexicali, recording a complex of remarks by Ava on the way as she stopped off for
an amazing variety of liquor while I drank only Cokes."

In Mexicali, they wandered around various bars. She
begged one couple to join them, but when they recognized her they became embarrassed and moved away. She
was furious when she saw a man behind a pillar trying to
photograph her. As the evening wore on she became
more and more annoyed with Hyams' probing questions:

she wanted to end the reporter-interviewee relationship and become friends, or more than that. But Hyams kept questioning her over and over again.

When he asked her if she had a guilt complex over her father's death, she threw a punch at him; he snatched the chair from under her and paddled her on the bottom. "Don't ever do that again!" he snapped. She seemed to enjoy the punishment, evidently pleased by his masculine self-assertion, and began to dance a flamenco.

By this time he was fiercely attracted to her. She suddenly suggested they check into a hotel: something cheap and seedy, which, she added, would still "seem beautiful at dawn." The invitation was brutally direct, but he declined it. He told her he would be so anxious to please her that he would fail her sexually. To fail with Ava Gardner would undoubtedly "destroy" his sexual self-confidence as a man, "which would give her something over him in the morning." "You son-of-a-bitch, you certainly know me, don't you?" she said sharply.

They drove all the way back to the house. Thereafter, over many meetings, Hyams heard from her details of her life, planning to write an authorized biography, which Ava later decided not to proceed with. Though there was a strong mutual attraction, they never had an affair.

That fall of 1954, Ava left by TWA for a promotional tour in the Orient for *The Barefoot Contessa*. She, Bappie, and David Hanna flew to Tokyo, where they stayed at the old Imperial Hotel, a maze of corridors like the inside of a pyramid. Much against her better judgment, she appeared on a stage at the opening of the film, stumbling through a speech in honor of Japan.

Donald Richie, best-known of American critics living in Tokyo, later told a story about Ava in those hectic few days: "She wanted to see a Japanese brothel," he said.

"So I took her to one. On a joke, she was to install herself in a room and I was to stand at the foot of the stairs and say to anyone who happened to be passing by, 'Ava Gardner's upstairs.' Well, a lot of girls were called 'Lana Turner' or 'Rita Hayworth' in those days if they wanted customers. So most men just wandered by, shaking their heads at this second-rate pimp's line of action.

"But finally a drunken American sailor came along. I said to him, 'Ava Gardner's upstairs. And she's cheap.' He went rolling along up the stairs. I thought, 'Well, at last something's going to happen.' Five minutes later he came running down the stairs white with horror. 'My God!' he yelled out. 'That *was* Ava Gardner!' "

Just before leaving, Ava sang for the troops—including two songs from *Show Boat*. The GIs loved the performance, and Ava was in a jubilant mood when she flew to Hong Kong and appeared cleverly decked out in a cheap Chinese dress at the premiere of *Contessa* there. It was a masterstroke of publicity, and the audience applauded her for it. In Singapore, she also made a strong impression. Then she flew to Europe—to Rome, Stockholm, and to London for *Contessa*'s British premiere.

Early in 1955, she was back in Madrid, but the affair with Dominguin was rapidly declining in intensity. He had envisaged a marriage with Ava, but now he was deeply conscious of the impossibility of this. In the first place, there was the severe opposition from his distinguished Catholic family, to whom he was devoted. In the second, Ava had failed to collect her divorce papers in Nevada, confirming his belief that she was still in love with Frank. If she had really meant to marry him, he would have risked public censure, but he knew she did not intend it. She remained, in the last analysis, a diverting physical affair, a gracious if difficult companion; and he was forced to see that the relationship could not possibly continue on a nonmarital basis.

Ava in her turn knew that she was not in love with Dominguin, that the stunning combination of looks, enormous wealth, intellect, and a respect for her had bowled her over. She decided to end the affair, but told Dominguin this with delicacy, consideration, and kindness. A little later, when he met and fell in love with a warm acquaintance of hers, the Italian star Lucia Bose, she accepted the situation with tender approval and concern for his future. It was one of her most admirable features as a woman that she continued to be friendly with the men she had been involved with.

That year, M-G-M was anxious for her to go to the Orient for the role of Victoria, a tormented Anglo-Indian, in a film version of John Masters' novel *Bhowani Junction*. The movie would be produced by Pandro S. Berman —"Pan" Berman was at this stage a good friend of hers —and directed by George Cukor, an extremely brilliant master craftsman whom she had liked at Metro, and who had a reputation for handling woman stars. The part of Victoria was well written: it expressed the divided feelings of a Eurasian in the period just after World War II in which Britain was gradually being dislodged from India. Clearly, this was a major opportunity to prove to herself and everyone else that she really might be able to act after all.

Since the movie dealt with the touchy subject of Anglo-Indian politics and featured a Eurasian as the leading figure, the Indian government refused to cooperate in the making. Berman applied in London, and the question was brought up in the Indian parliament, but permission was completely ruled out.

Pakistan gave permission immediately, and Berman settled on Lahore as the location. The whole unit and cast, Ava included, flew in and stayed at Felatti's Hotel in Lahore.

Berman remembers Ava at that time: "Ava was no longer the beautiful child that came from the farm. She was a woman now, she had bags under her eyes. She was pretty distraught over money, she had been in the business for 14 years and she had no money to show for it. She had spent every cent.

"We had dinner in her suite one night, just the two of us. We had a long discussion and I gave her a lot of advice. I told her she should start to save her money, to stop squandering it. I frightened the hell out of her. It was probably the first time in her life that anyone dared to tell her the truth."

Felatti's was a horrible hotel, shabby and depressing, a low, rambling structure, with additional buildings like hovels. Ava's rooms were little better than the rest. A living room was separated from the bedroom by a curtain. There was no electric fan or air conditioner. On the back step, on the edge of a dirty yard, a servant slept. The food was atrocious, with violently flavored curries. The heat was stifling, over 100 degrees with high humidity. Not even the experience of making *Ride, Vaquero* was as terrible as this.

During the first few days an incident out of a nightmare took place. Pandro Berman, Ava, and several others were having "tiffin" or afternoon tea on the lawn outside the hotel, when they became aware of a strange rustling sound in the trees above their heads. Berman looked up and saw a mass of black things forming a cloud in the branches. The rustling increased and wings suddenly spread against the sky. A moment later Berman told Ava and the others to duck. The birds—enormous carrion crows—swooped down, flapping in everyone's face, and plucked every scrap of food off the table.

Nearly everyone was ill during the making of the picture. Sleep was virtually impossible, and medical help haphazard. Phones, electricity, and gas failed to work. There was no night life. George Cukor coldly shrugs off the experience. "All picture-making is hell," he says.

But Pandro Berman is more frank: "It was horrendous, all of it. I don't know how we got through it alive."

Much of the shooting took place in streets where the excrement of humans and animals drifted along the gutters or poured out of open drains.

Ava was determined not to let her horror and disgust at the environment show in her behavior. Moreover, her extraordinary will power pulled her through when nearly everyone else was down with various forms of dysentery from the food. Supplies of canned goods had to be flown in from Hollywood, but still the violent stomach disorders and fevers continued. Only Ava remained sturdy and virtually untouched by illness.

"Ava was a gem," George Cukor says. "She was marvelously punctual and never complained even when it was clear the poor darling was *exhausted*. She was wonderful in the part."

Berman says: "She simply wasn't dating anyone at that time. People kept trying to link her with Bill Travers, who also played a Eurasian in the picture, but that was ridiculous. I'd heard about her promiscuity, but I found her amazingly chaste. Maybe she was too tired to do anything except work."

Ava went to bed—alone and early—each night and felt she had achieved something important in the playing of the part. But to her bitter disappointment—and Cukor's —the film was subjected to a laundering process by M-G-M which virtually ruined it. Nevertheless, Ava's performance as Victoria—anguished, vulnerable, torn by conflicts—was among the most effective of her career, and the critics were kind.

Back from Pakistan, Ava completed some interior scenes of *Bhowani Junction* in London and finally settled in Spain in December 1955. She found a house she liked and moved in on December 20, a few days before her thirty-third birthday, after paying $50,000 for the house and $25,000 for redecorations and furnishings. It was a handsome red brick chalet with two acres of ground in La Moraleja, a luxurious colony a few miles out of the city in a small wood. In those days La Moraleja was known as "The Beverly Hills of Spain." The house was one of a hundred or so occupied mostly by Americans. It was extremely beautiful, with a lush garden. The interior was comfortable and chic without seeming "decorated"; Ava worked out the design herself, with the aid of her close friend the decorator Harris Williams, and she hung the walls with her favorite paintings—18th century English landscape masterpieces bought at Sotheby's auctions in London, Spanish abstracts by Viola, Quiró, and Saura.

Her furnishings were simple and quiet: polished mahogany and walnut, including a magnificent and elegant dining room suite. In the living room was her one open touch of vanity: alongside the landscapes and the abstracts, a large M-G-M publicity portrait of Ava from the old days, blown up and handsomely framed. Nearby on a table stood a nude statue of her. The library was crowded with scores of books; by this time Ava had become a voracious reader. The scripts of her films were bound in handsome leather, with gold titles printed on the spines. In the cellar she kept two gigantic trunks full of professional souvenirs—tape recordings of the sound tracks of her films, photographs, old clothes—and a staggering collection of records, some 10,000 of them. Her favorites were the Sinatra records, many of them collectors' items, and she had three of each of these, because often in haste or if she had drunk too much she would scratch records or leave them lying on the floor.

Known as La Bruja or "The Witch," because of an iron weathervane shaped like a witch on a broomstick, the house deeply involved Ava for a time. But she was as restless as ever. She went to bullfights in Seville and Malaga; she visited the gypsies, to whom she was warm and generous, enjoying their beautiful dances in caves; she traveled north to the San Fermin *corrida*, to Pamplona (that favorite setting of Hemingway novels), to San Sebastian (with a quick and easy crossover to Biarritz in France and its then fashionable beach), and to other fashionable, tourist-crowded places. She learned to speak Spanish fluently, with only a touch of accent, and rejoiced in the crude, blasphemous, and "dirty" words of the various provincial regions. She only used Spanish when necessary for traveling, shopping, or dealing with craftsmen and artists. With her American or British friends, she spoke only English, and she usually flattered her Spanish friends by talking to them in English as well.

She seldom went to the theater in Spain and took no interest in Spanish cinema or serious music. Since American films were dubbed she very seldom went to these either.

She enjoyed the night life in Madrid: drinks with *tapas* (small dishes of food) in *tascos* (small taverns), instead of visits to the more sophisticated *mesones* (old-fashioned inns), where the middle-class citizens of the city liked to spend their evenings. From the *tascos*, she and her set—usually seven or eight people—would go on to dinner or to the *tablaos flamencos*, nightclubs with flamenco dancing and drinks, until they were asked to leave at about 4 a.m., or in some cases were forcibly pushed—laughing or

angry—into the street. On some occasions she would ask
for a particular small club to be reopened especially for
her, or would go to places at 5 a.m. for chocolate and
churros (fried paste), or would have the whole group go
in a succession of taxis to her house, where the dancing
and drinking would continue until 10 a.m.

Ava never saw a check on these occasions: someone
always picked up the tab. Often a famous nightclub—the
Oliver for instance—simply didn't charge her at all because of the fame or notoriety she could bring to the
establishment. Her friends in Madrid were few, among
them the writer H. M. Herbert, her neighbors the Richard
Sicres (she adored Betty Sicre), the Portuguese actor
Virgilio Teixeira, the designer Harris Williams, and, in
particular, Perico Chicote, the famous millionaire bartender.

The widespread belief that Ava "found" herself in
Spain and discovered happiness and personal security
there is totally groundless. The myth was launched by the
Spanish themselves in order to attract tourists to a
country which had been politically cut off and despised
for its neutrality, spiritually disliked, and geographically
underestimated.

When Ava had first arrived in 1950, the era of ration-
ing had barely ended and the country was still recovering
from the effects of a long period of isolation during the
war. Ava, discovering herself to be the first international
star to live in Spain, was enormously pleased and flattered. "She felt heavenly," a male Spanish friend of that
time who wishes to be anonymous says today. "Only later
she realized she was being used and abused for other
people's interests, and that tourism was exploiting her.
Suddenly she stopped talking publicly about her love of
the country. In time she found that the Spanish were not

as sweet, disinterested, and joyful as she thought. She learned resentment at our big bluff."

Despite her serious effort to adapt, Ava remained very American in Madrid. She enjoyed the sunshine, the vitality and earnestness of the common people, the cheap drinks. She reveled in singing and dancing, spending the night combing the streets for new drinking bars, and above all the mealtimes, which coincided with her body clock: lunch at 3 p.m., dinner at 11 p.m., supper at 2 a.m. Unlike those other Hispanophiles, Hemingway and Orson Welles, she did not enjoy obscure regional dishes, salads, shellfish, and special vegetables, and in fact shunned all Spanish food with two exceptions: newborn eels (anguilas a la Bilbaina) and paella. Instead, she preferred American steaks, hamburgers, and Italian food— pasta ciuta, parmigiano cheese, and imported Italian tomatoes. She loved to cook spaghetti, tagliatella, and lasagna. Despite the fact that she often had a cook in her employ, she prepared dinners herself for small groups of friends. She liked Spanish drinks, including anis del mono or sol y sombra (half anise and half Spanish cognac mixed), sherrys and various liqueurs, gin mixed with beer, bourbon—almost never Scotch—and champagne.

She also liked to drive, very fast, a fact which caused her to overturn her Mercedes in the streets of Madrid on two occasions, though she emerged uninjured and with nothing more serious than a speeding ticket.

Chapter 11

I N 1956, AVA WAS for the most part resident in Madrid, where Sinatra came in the spring months to make a film for Stanley Kramer, *The Pride and the Passion*. She was still legally married to him, since she had failed to sit out the necessary waiting period in Nevada. Though she was through with him, she was horrified when he arrived in Madrid with a starlet, Peggy Connolly. She told her friends exactly what she thought of him, and what he could do with the car he had sent her so ostentatiously for Christmas. When they ran into each other in restaurants, she pointedly ignored him, and on one occasion she even rose from her table and walked out.

She was aggravated that spring not only by Frank's

reappearance but by the attention paid to her by the Dominican playboy Porfirio Rubirosa, who on the basis of two brief meetings in Madrid and Paris kept insisting that they were having an affair and would be married in the summer—a story printed by the *New York Journal-American* columnist Cholly Knickerbocker.

In the wake of Dominguin, Ava began dating a handsome young Italian actor, Walter Chiari. Thirty year old Chiari was known as the "Danny Kaye of Italy." He had been one of the country's most celebrated comedy stars since 1946. Born in Verona, raised in Milan, and trained in the navy, he had first been acclaimed as a romantic comedian when he appeared in a theatrical group touring Italy in 1948. Since that time, he had starred in some 42 movies, including several with the celebrated Italian clown Toto. Chiari was truly Ava's type: lean, hard, bronzed, masculine, with narrow hips. He was adorably witty, modest, unassuming, kind. The combination of good looks and humor was intoxicating. Nevertheless, it seems certain that Ava never really fell in love with Chiari, any more than she had with Howard Duff. From the outset, it was a one-sided relationship, that brutal fact disguised in the apparent joy, freedom, and openness of their association.

I talked to Chiari about Ava in Sydney, Australia, in 1967, over various interviews on and off the set of a comedy, *They're a Weird Mob*, in which he appeared as a new Italian immigrant puzzled by the peculiar customs of Australian people. Always with a pretty girl or two in attendance, always laughing, he exuded optimism even on crowded, inefficient sets, surrounded by extras and electricians, under the burning arcs or the scorching Australian sun. He spoke of Ava with such warmth and understanding one wonders why she didn't marry him. He says: "The problem was that Ava was an interna-

tional star of the first magnitude, whereas I was not
known outside of Italy. My income was very small by her
standards. It was true that Frank Sinatra and Artie Shaw
were not successful at the time she met them, and that
they attracted her motherly instincts as well as her
masochism. But they had been international figures, and
they would be again. I think she felt I was 'riding on her
coattails,' that I was using her to improve my chances of
professional success. This was odd, because she had always resented the fact that people accused her of riding
on Mickey Rooney's coattails—and she was right: it was
a gross libel of her.

"For the most part, Ava and I were happy together.
But I don't believe she ever totally and committedly loved
me as I loved her. I was obsessed with her. She was the
most beautiful woman I had ever known. Yet somehow
when we were together I often felt I was alone, that she
had withdrawn from me in some mysterious and unset-
tling way, and that it was going to be impossible for me to
fulfill her, and this was a very severe blow to my Italian
male ego.

"I don't want to give the impression though that ours
was always a strained and unhappy relationship. We
shared so many things in common. She had a passion for
Italian food, for Rome, for things Italian. She had a
wonderful sense of humor, making fun of herself and
others, and I loved her for that as much as for anything
else. We traveled together, shopped together, slept together, most of the time in perfect harmony. I was enormously proud of her. But I still had the nagging feeling I
could never possess her. The only one who 'possessed'
Ava Gardner was that adorable Ava herself."

To judge by the written accounts of her press agent
and others, Chiari's judgment of the relationship was
shrewd and accurate. Ava was constantly torn between

admiring Walter and feeling great affectionate amusement and warmth toward him, and dreading the possibility that he might be dating her only in order to turn himself into an international star. It was not until later that she learned of his complete and obsessed devotion: enslaved by her totally, he put up with her fits of temper, followed her wherever she went, even (according to press agent David Hanna) humiliating himself to please her. She almost certainly resented this, yet, in her contradictory soul, adored the devotion as well.

A particular thorn in Walter's side in the first period of their relationship was that Frank Sinatra was in and out of Madrid. Despite their differences, Ava rejoiced in Frank's enormous new professional success: after *From Here to Eternity*, he had made a string of very successful movies, he had left Columbia for Capitol Records, with major results in terms of popularity; he no longer struggled through half-attended performances, but enjoyed packed houses; he had signed a $9 million television contract for shows on the ABC network. Yet Ava's enthusiasm for Frank's great triumphs did not, as Walter thought, signify any rekindling of the relationship. They were virtually strangers now, and their passion for each other was extinguished for good; even when, later on, they became the close friends they are today, there was no going back to their sexual relationship.

Asked at the time to comment on her relationships, Ava said: "I have an affinity for jerks. But that won't stop me looking for the right man. Every time I fall in love, or think I'm in love, I'll get married. I will try and make the best of my marriage, but I think I'll die if another marriage fails. And if I don't die, I'll kill myself."

A firm friendship Ava established early in 1956 was with the British poet and literary critic Robert Graves,

who lived in Majorca. At the suggestion of a mutual
friend, she flew into Palma, where Graves met her in a
Landrover. She was so besieged by fans that, Graves reported later, she had to keep changing hotels. She was dismayed by the simple British food eaten at the Graves'
home, much preferring to take her host and hostess out at
night. But she was caught by the beauty of his *Collected
Poems*, and especially by one he singled out for her: it told
of someone who was "wild and innocent," someone who
would love "through all disaster."

Ava enjoyed Majorca enormously, and liked swimming
in the icy water at Campo del Mar, tasting wine in the
vineyards, talking for hours to Graves about poetry and
the Greek and Roman legends.

"She was sensitive, subdued, at once tragic and adorable," Graves says. "She wanted to drink life down."
They were to become great friends in future years.

Much to Ava's annoyance that year, she was still under
contract to M-G-M. After turning down both *Love Me or
Leave Me*—a decision she later regretted, because it made
a major dramatic star out of Doris Day—and a ridiculous
Mexican subject, *Fiesta*, she had been given a number of
other scripts she had refused to make. Finally, she
shrugged and agreed to appear in a second-rate romantic
comedy, *The Little Hut*, which was based on the silly
premise that three healthy men on a desert island would
not make love to a woman who looked like Ava Gardner.
The play, which showed each of the men sharing the
woman in turn, had at least been rational smut, but as
usual M-G-M cleaned the story up and ruined it. Ava was
repelled by the script, and felt that the only real chance
for enjoyment in making the picture would be that an old
acquaintance she very much liked, David Niven, was in

it. And Walter Chiari was in the film as a native on the island.

Just before she began work on *The Little Hut* in Rome, Ava granted a rare interview to Ruth Waterbury, her first hostess in Hollywood. She sat in the corner of a dark bar at the Castellana Hilton in Madrid. Attacking M-G-M bitterly, saying that her part in *The Little Hut* was going to be "lousy" (when the statement was published, M-G-M was furious), and dismissing coldly Ruth's questions about Lord Jimmy Grenville, with whom the columnists falsely linked her (she had met him with friends in London), she refused to discuss her supposed affairs with bullfighters. When Ruth praised her for *Bhowani Junction* she said exhaustedly, "Why didn't they take the close-ups of me at the beginning instead of the end of the picture, when I was worn out by the location? They always do the wrong thing in this lousy business." She told a little story: "I got lost on my way to my doctor's. Suddenly a crowd of street kids came by and recognized me. They led me all the way to the doctor! I felt like the Pied Piper of Hamelin!"

Regretting that she had given the interview—she always hated giving them, but felt she owed Ruth Waterbury a favor—Ava shortly afterward flew to Rome to start work on *The Little Hut*. The script depressed her more and more; and she found the Cinecitta Studio set, supposed to represent a desert island, absurd. In the vast, chilly studio, she was supposed to sit around in Dorothy Lamour-like tropical clothes, while she played cat-and-mouse with her fellow actors. Walter Chiari was even worse off: he appeared as the native in heavy tan makeup, in a loincloth, trying to emote a ridiculous part to which he was totally unsuited.

Back in Madrid in the late fall of 1956, Ava had a

letter from Henry King, who had excited her admiration when they made *The Snows of Kilimanjaro* together four years earlier. He enclosed a treatment by Peter Viertel based on Hemingway's *The Sun Also Rises*, and offered her the role of the tragic and dissolute Lady Brett. She had always wanted to play in another Hemingway film, and had often thought of asking M-G-M to buy *A Farewell to Arms* for her from Paramount.

The Sun Also Rises had originally been bought for $10,000 by RKO-Radio Pictures in 1930, but had never reached the screen. The rights had been transferred by Hemingway to his first wife, Hadley, in a divorce settlement. In 1947, Charles Feldman bought the rights for $35,000 from the actor Harry Banister, who had obtained them for his wife, Ann Harding, an actress with a long-standing desire to play Lady Brett. In 1955, 20th Century-Fox obtained the rights, at a figure of $125,000, and finally overcame the censorship objections to the impotence of the hero, Jake Barnes, who was to be played by Tyrone Power.

Although Ava had her doubts about again playing a woman involved with an impotent man ("Maybe the public will think I make men impotent," a columnist in Spain quoted her as saying), she decided to go ahead, and M-G-M—reluctantly as always—agreed to loan her out to 20th Century-Fox once more.

Ava had been Henry King's only choice for the role of Lady Brett. "And I don't mean because she had had an affair with a bullfighter and lived in Spain," he said. "She had that moving, haunted, 'crying out' quality. No one else could have done it, and it was the best thing she ever did."

King had been completely satisfied with her playing of Cynthia in *The Snows of Kilimanjaro*, his only reservation being that her voice was too thin and needed deepen-

Left: With Robert Taylor in
Ride, Vaquero (M-G-M).
Opposite: With Clark Gable
in *Mogambo* (UNITED PRESS
INTERNATIONAL PHOTO)

Below: With Donald Sinden, Grace Kelly, Clark Gable, and
Philip Stainton in *Mogambo* (M-G-M)

Above: With Mel Ferrer in a scene from *Knights of the Round Table* (M-G-M). *Below:* With Humphrey Bogart in *The Barefoot Contessa* (UNITED ARTISTS)

The barefoot dance in *The Barefoot Contessa*
(UNITED PRESS INTERNATIONAL PHOTO)

Ava Gardner in *Bhowani Junction* (M-G-M)

Above: On the set of *Bhowani Junction* in Pakistan with Stewart Granger seeking shade from the 110 degree heat (M-G-M). *Below:* With bullfighter Luis Miguel Dominguin at ringside (WIDE WORLD PHOTOS)

Left: Ava in costume for *The Little Hut* (M-G-M). *Below*: With Walter Chiari in a romantic scene from *The Little Hut* (UNITED PRESS INTERNATIONAL PHOTO)

With Eddie Albert, Errol Flynn, Mel Ferrer, and Tyrone Power
in *The Sun Also Rises* (20TH CENTURY-FOX)

ing. So he asked her to go into the garden of La Bruja and read aloud, over and over again, certain favorite passages from books. This she did. But when he sent her the first draft screenplay she was appalled at its infidelity to the novel and took it to Hemingway. He was equally devastated and cabled Darryl Zanuck that he would sue if the book were distorted in this fashion. King asked Peter Viertel, who was in England, to rewrite the material, and after some weeks King flew by the polar route to London to work with Viertel. Finally they had a script which more or less met with Hemingway's satisfaction.

Mary Hemingway remembers Ava in 1956: "Ava and Ernest and I went to bullfights together. Ernest was very fond of her. She was one of the few dames we met during our marriage who didn't want to go to bed with Ernest. She didn't make passes at him the way other women did. She was almost unique. Almost everyone else tried to get him into bed. I could understand this, because he was very nice in bed.

"I liked her very much. We didn't necessarily have any great intellectual rapport, but I didn't find her stupid. In Spain, she was fascinated by bullfighting and learned quite a bit about it. She wasn't interested in writing, literature, which interested me a lot. Ava liked music. Not particularly classical.

"She didn't stay at our house in Cuba, but we went fishing. I have an awfully cute picture of her in the back of our boat, the *Pilar*. When we'd be going fishing in the harbor of Havana Bay, everybody would look at her with admiration, and I suppose some degree of wishing they could chat with her. Our chauffeur was in love with her. He was as black as a black olive. And so was our butler. They were all in love with her, but wouldn't say so.

"She was always very nice to me, unlike most of the

other women around Ernest. She was always well mannered. Ernest called her 'daughter' and patted her on the
head and stuff like that. She called him Papa, as we all
did. We both thought she was a nice girl, and he thought
she was beautiful, natch. She was restless and irritable
and I said, 'You know Ava, if you could just enjoy reading, it would give you such an enormous pleasure.' Ernest
would sort of agree with that. I recall saying something of
that sort to her."

In November 1956, Ava flew to London to conclude
the contractual agreements on *The Sun Also Rises*, then
left for a vacation in the south of France. She swept aside
rumors that she was going to marry Walter Chiari, pointing out that she was still technically married to Frank.
She said that when she went to Mexico to make the film
that December (Spain having been ruled out because of
the severe winter), she would probably obtain a Mexican
divorce. A few days later she denied she would ever seek
a divorce at all. Her indecision over the final break with
Frank clearly agonized her—and Chiari even more.

Early in 1957, the picture some weeks behind schedule,
Ava left for Mexico City—without Walter, who was busy
with screen and stage engagements in Italy and did not
arrive until May. In the meantime, she was seen frequently with screenwriter Peter Viertel, the handsome
and brilliant son of Garbo's close friend, screenwriter
Salka Viertel. Friends agree that theirs was a largely intellectual relationship, that Ava was overawed by Viertel's
extraordinary intelligence. It is doubtful if they had, as
many gossips suggested, a passionate affair.

King had begun shooting bullfights in Pamplona,
Spain, but the bitter snow made it impossible to proceed
with the body of the action, and so the entire film was
scheduled to be made in Morelia, Mexico, where the bullring was repainted as a copy of its Pamplona counterpart.

In Morelia, the company, headed by Ava, Tyrone Power, Mel Ferrer, and Errol Flynn, moved into hotels, though Ava asked for and got the use of a beautiful house near the Aqueduct, with a hairdresser and a maid. Later, in Mexico City, she occupied a magnificent suite of rooms at the Hotel Bamer, with a spiral staircase leading to the bedroom. When King told her the staircase looked precarious—he was thinking of her drinking—she threw back her head and roared with laughter.

Night after night, she partied until dawn with groups of friends, and yet morning after morning she somehow managed to get onto the set in time. King remembers: "One morning she announced that she was feeling under the weather and wouldn't be at the Chapultepec Castle filming that day. Shooting was scheduled to start at 1 p.m. Zanuck brought the news to me and I said, 'She'll *be* there.' I let it be known that Metro would be sued if she failed to turn up as she was on loan-out from them. I absolutely refused to listen to her absurd behavior. Once she heard that I was unshaken, I guess she was shocked into action. She crept up behind me while I ate lunch, put a pair of cool hands over my eyes, and said, sweetly, 'You should be ashamed. A one o'clock call and you haven't finished your lunch!' After that, shooting proceeded without mishap."

King says it was the happiest company he ever worked with. He, Ava, and her co-stars Errol Flynn and Mel Ferrer met at the Hotel Bamer for dinner as a group, and when they were in Morelia, Ava, would also go out of her way to mingle with Flynn and the others. She acted with distinction under King's scrupulously considerate direction.

By all accounts, Ava enormously enjoyed her weeks in Morelia and Mexico City. She hated leaving the house in Morelia, with its 15 rooms, blue-tiled swimming pool, and leafy gardens. She liked playing tennis and swimming with Peter Viertel. During breaks in shooting at various locations and at the Curubusco Studios in Mexico City, she played tennis at the country club with Walter (who imagined she was having an affair with Tyrone Power, though in fact she did not even get along with him), and went shopping with Nicole Fontana, her Roman dress designer, and Audrey Hepburn, wife of Mel Ferrer.

Jim Nelson, a visitor to the set, noted, "She gave parties constantly for the Ferrers, whom she liked enormously."

Bob Evans, cast as the romantic bullfighter, played a scene with her that might have been out of Ava's real life, and told reporter Favius Friedman: "Ava was wonderful after we got over the first hurdle. When she's in a scene she shoots off electrical sparks. Our love scene was so violent that when it ended my teeth were chattering, and she took a half hour rest!"

Mr. Evans, later the production head of Paramount, told me in his office in Beverly Hills: "I had a real collision with Ava at the outset of the picture. She had determined that Walter Chiari would play the bullfighter. Zanuck and Henry King wanted me. So she was rude and unpleasant to me—which made our love scenes an ordeal. But later on she relented, and became reasonably friendly. She drank far, far too much, her language disgusted me in a woman, and I thought her sister was a bad influence on her. When we ran into each other at parties later we were always nice to each other. But that early bitterness remained."

When the shooting of *The Sun Also Rises* was completed, Ava left for Hollywood with an entourage which included Bappie, Nicole Fontana, Walter Chiari, and

Peter Viertel; she stayed at the Nichols Canyon house, which she had given to Bappie.

Reporter Favius Friedman, who followed her doggedly in this period, wrote: "There were only a few days in Hollywood, and a few gay nights. One evening she danced her favorite flamenco with her old companion Peter Viertel at the Club Seville, and the next night she was back again, this time with Chiari, dancing more hours through." She shunned interviews, looked terrified between dances, shielding her face behind menus, and when she emerged in daylight to do some shopping, wore enormous dark glasses and a Garboesque head scarf which, of course, made her more conspicuous than ever. Then she flew to Havana to see the Hemingways, and on to Madrid, the red brick La Bruja and the tall iron gates.

There, she rested quietly, seeing few people apart from the Sicres, and reading scripts. One of these interested her: it was based on the career of Conchita Cintron, the famous lady bullfighter.

She talked extensively to a friend, Tamara Lewe, a South African woman who had acquired a local reputation as a female torero. Ava wanted to try her own hand at bullfighting; the idea, somewhat dismaying her friends, grew to an obsession, and in October she paid a visit to the ranch of Angel Peralta, the celebrated trainer of bulls for the *corrida*, near Seville. It was there that an incident took place which was to alter the whole tenor of Ava Gardner's life.

A very distinguished man of great wealth and position, Peralta was at once amused and delighted by Ava's latest ambition. He decided to indulge her, though some of his friends criticized him for "spoiling a tourist," and he arranged for her a special demonstration of *toreo a caballo*, the technique of fighting bulls on horseback. Peralta offered her one of his finest horses to ride, and a special

lance to taunt the bull. She immediately accepted the
challenge. A bull charged violently at her and she struck
it with the rubber-tipped lance. As she did so, her horse
reared, she pulled the reins, and was badly thrown; she
tried to rise to her feet and the bull charged directly at
her. She was able to throw up one arm to protect most of
her face, but the bull struck one cheek and threw her into
the air. She screamed and broke into tears as Peralta's
men chased the bull away.

Ava was lifted onto a chair and carried into the ranch
house, crying hysterically. Peralta's staff stuffed ice into
her swollen cheeks, but when she looked into a mirror
she discovered that one side of her face had been damaged. For her this was the ultimate horror: her one unas-
sailable stock-in-trade, her beauty, might be ruined, and
her career, which she had so long pretended to despise,
might be finished for good.

Friends in Seville told her to fly at once to London to
see the specialist Sir Archibald McIndoe, a plastic sur-
geon with a fine reputation for work on temperamental
stars. She was on a plane the following day. McIndoe told
her he could do nothing; that in time the swelling—
medically known as a hematoma—would go down and
she must simply sit out the ordeal. She vomited and was
hysterical and had to lie down for long periods. She
shunned all public appearances except a brief opening of
McIndoe's new hospital, which was an unhappy experience for her. From that moment on, she had a deep-
seated terror of photographs and publicity.

She became even more obsessed with her face than
before. Her insecurities emerged more drastically than
ever. Her obsession to earn enough money to protect
herself in her later years was overpowering. In the wake
of the terrible shock the incident had given her—remind-
ing her of the impermanence of beauty, of mortality and

the inevitable progress of age—Ava was torn by two conflicting impulses. One was that she must harvest every
cent for the future by taking any film role which happened to be offered to her; the other that she must retire
from the screen at once, that she must never again be
seen in public. She managed somehow to resolve these
conflicts, first by taking a succession of parts which did
her little credit but bolstered her precarious financial position, second by giving fewer and fewer interviews and
permitting almost no photographers.

The tragedy was that all this personal suffering was
totally unnecessary, based on a deep neurosis. The mark
on her cheek was almost invisible to the naked eye, even
when she was not wearing makeup, though some keen-
eyed women humiliated her at parties by commenting on
the "bluish marks on her face." Only on the minutest
examination did a shadow show on the slight rising of the
surface of the skin in one place. But the mirror told her
otherwise: in her eyes, the mark was large, hideous,
permanently disfiguring. She began to cry uncontrollably,
and her drinking, always a defense against fear, began to
be very serious indeed, endangering even her robust
health and aging her rapidly.

The effects of the trauma at Peralta's ranch were in-
calculable in every aspect of her behavior. She grew more
and more erratic and unpredictable. At 36, she began to
have all of the nervous querulousness of a much older
woman. Her violent temper worsened by the month. Her
language became more and more coarse. Yet she still had
much of the old humor, generosity, and vitality; her sense
of fun still served to captivate Hemingway and Robert
Graves.

It was out of desperation and fear of the future that,
toward the end of 1957, living at La Bruja with her corgi

dogs, still quarreling and making up with Walter Chiari, Ava reluctantly agreed to play a role long planned for her: that of the willful Duchess of Alba in a film version of the life of Goya, *The Naked Maja*. It was to be produced by Goffredo Lombardo in the summer of 1958. For five years, Lombardo had planned to make the movie, and had tried unsuccessfully to buy the rights to Lion Feuchtwanger's novel about the painter, *This Is the Hour*.

A stack of scripts had been prepared, but there were endless delays until a merger of Titanus Productions and United Artists, and a distribution guarantee by M-G-M based on Ava's acceptance of the pivotal role, made the project possible. Lombardo settled on Madrid for filming, and chose Henry Koster as director.

The idea of making the picture in Madrid appealed to Ava very strongly: she would not have to undertake the ordeal of travel to a foreign country, with all that implied in swarming fans, photographers, and face-to-face interviews. But repeated complaints from the still powerful descendants of the Duchess of Alba resulted in a refusal on the part of the Franco government to permit the picture to be made anywhere in Spain. Lombardo was forced to transfer the production to Rome.

Still haunted by the fear of the hematoma showing up on the screen, Ava left for Rome in May 1958. Walter Chiari followed her from Madrid like a pet dog but she quarreled with him, accusing him unfairly of exploiting her for his own gain. When she arrived at the Titanus Studios, she had constant arguments over costumes and with her lighting cameraman, the great Giuseppe Rotunno. She looked haggard, with dark circles under her eyes, and Rotunno had to contrive ingenious filters to soften her exhausted look.

There was further trouble when her co-star Anthony

Franciosa arrived to play Goya, accompanied by his wife, Shelley Winters. Franciosa, intense and passionately committed, had flung himself with characteristic drive into studying for the role of the painter. For months he had been reading biographies, examining Goya's paintings, and traveling from one end of Spain to another seeking out Goya's haunts.

According to both Henry Koster and Shelley Winters, he steeped himself so totally in the part that he "became" the neurotic, tension-ridden painter, so overwrought that he vomited before scenes, screamed at the director, and made life hell for the producer. According to Shelley Winters, "Ava wrung him dry, she made love to him, he was sick and exhausted, he lost weight." According to Henry Koster, "Franciosa and Ava hated each other. They used to sulk in separate dressing rooms between scenes, refusing to speak to each other." As well as refereeing these serious conflicts, Koster, an experienced commercial film craftsman better known for his Deanna Durbin pictures than for film dramas, quarreled with the slow and lackadaisical Roman crew, which hated his Germanic authority. In a rare and brief interview with a newspaper, Ava told Robert F. Hawkins of *The New York Times*, "The one decent thing about this job is that it's my last picture under the Metro contract. I'll be free in September."

Tony Franciosa told me about the depressing experience at a party given by Merv Griffin for Rita Hayworth in 1971. "I worked like hell on that picture," he said. "And what did I get for it? The worst notices of my entire career. Ava? Well those stories everyone, including Shelley, put about that we were having an affair are so damn ridiculous I'm not going to insult you by even bothering to take them seriously. Ava and I were thrust together in an unworkable situation with a director who was wrong for the subject, and a production team which didn't know what the fuck it was doing. So what do you expect? That I'm climbing into bed with Ava every five minutes? We acted together because we had to. I respected what she could do, she respected what I could do, and by the end of the movie all we wanted to do was get out and forget the whole stupid mess we'd gotten ourselves into."

Back in Rome, stories of clashes between Ava and Shelley Winters over Ava's supposed infatuation with Franciosa were widely publicized, especially an account of a hair-pulling, glass-throwing struggle in a bar in Rome in which the two women battled over their man. "They said I pulled her hair out at the roots!" Shelley Winters fumes today. "That whole story is a complete lie. The fact is that Ava was chasing after Tony on the picture. He was so unsettled by her that he had to have a rest and we closed down the picture for two weeks. I took him to Anacapri, the hilly region above Capri, to recuperate, and Ava followed him. She put out a story that I was keeping my husband a prisoner. So just to spite her I put out a story that I had fought with her over Tony and pulled out her hair. Then people would think she had no hair and wouldn't use her! It was sweet revenge!"

Ava aggravated Koster and Lombardo by insisting that the entire picture could easily be made at night; she refused to work before 6 p.m. Then, the moment the shooting was over, she flew to London for another examination of the hematoma.

Back in Rome, she worked for weeks on dubbing sessions, while at the same time reading and re-reading a new script she had agreed to film: Stanley Kramer's *On the Beach*, based on the novel by Nevil Shute. Kramer had flown to Rome to discuss her part with her: that of a heavy-drinking Australian party girl who is one of the last survivors of an atomic war.

In his office at Columbia Pictures in 1965, Stanley Kramer said: "She simply failed to turn up to our first meeting. The second day she did turn up and I was impressed by how deeply she understood her role—not intellectually but with a sensitive and humane intuition. Next time I tried to discuss the material with her she seemed more interested in dancing a flamenco."

But they established a rapport, and even though they constantly argued later on, they retained a profound mutual respect.

Ava found Kramer's screenplay moving, and wanted to play the part more than any since Victoria in *Bhowani Junction*. After a brief trip to Paris, and more quarrels there with Walter, she returned to Rome to prepare for the trip to Australia. When her costumes were ready, she traveled to London, where Sir Archibald McIndoe performed a small operation to remove what trace of the hematoma was still visible.

The Naked Maja was a box-office disaster which everyone connected with it would today prefer to forget. But the misery of its completion was softened by Ava's interest in *On the Beach*, and by the good notices she received for her role of Lady Brett in *The Sun Also Rises*. One dissentient about that picture (though he admired Ava as always) was Ernest Hemingway, according to columnist Art Buchwald, who interviewed him in Paris. Sitting in a green bathrobe at the Hotel George V, Hemingway told Buchwald: "I saw Darryl Zanuck's splashy Cook's tour of Europe's lost generation: bistros, bullfights, and more bistros. It's all pretty disappointing, and that's being gracious. You're meant to be in Spain and all you see walking around are Mexicans. Pretty silly."

Zanuck snarled a retort: "A lousy thing to say. He doesn't have the right to destroy publicly something he's been paid for." Zanuck added: "I don't think he saw the picture. I think someone told him about it." He was right. That someone was certainly Ava herself, who was quoted as saying, "What happened to Hemingway shouldn't happen to a dog."

Chapter 12

WITH AVA FIRMLY SIGNED, Stanley Kramer began assembling the cast and crew for *On the Beach* in America and Europe. Gregory Peck was chosen to play the submarine commander who in a final reconnaissance from Melbourne to San Francisco discovers that the rest of the world has been destroyed. Fred Astaire agreed to play a nondancing role as a scientist, and Anthony Perkins a young naval officer. A team of reporters went to cover the shooting, including Ruth Waterbury, who traveled on the plane with Ava's party for the *New York Daily News*.

Meanwhile, Kramer moved into Melbourne, where he was dismayed to find there were no film-making facilities.

Australia, with half of its theater chains owned by 20th Century-Fox and the other half part-owned by J. Arthur Rank in Great Britain, had not for years had a decent film studio. What little equipment was available had been snatched up by a British company making a film called *The Summer of the Seventeenth Doll* in Sydney. "I had to build a studio from the ground up," Kramer says. "I had to find a submarine and an aircraft carrier. Practically everything had to be flown in from the States: a racing car, my mobile generators, the dressing rooms for the stars. Then, when we started in on preliminary shooting, huge crowds came to watch us. I guess we were the first exciting thing that happened in Melbourne since the dawn of creation."

Ava arrived in Sydney on the afternoon of January 5, 1959, looking remarkably composed and assured. Despite the sticky humid heat of the Australian summer, she seemed cool in her black Fontana suit, her white blouse and gloves, and she answered a barrage of reporters' idiotic and predictable questions without rancor. She seemed rattled only when a writer for the *Sydney Sun* asked her, "Did your face get injured at a party in Madrid?" She looked at the man icily, without answering, forcing him to say awkwardly, "It was probably very ungallant of me." She smiled and brushed him off with the words, "Yes, very ungallant."

She dismissed any mention of her affair with Walter, but made it clear she was still "very close" to Mickey, Artie, and Frank. She laughed loudly when a woman asked her if she "liked late nights and high living." Startled by the rather foolish and naive, but on the whole well-meaning, questions, and frankly pleased by the fresh, open-faced people who stood on cars and trucks to cheer and even to salute her as she went by, she changed planes for Melbourne in rare good humor.

The trouble started when she got to Melbourne and began filming. The heat was severe—almost as severe as that she had experienced in Utah, Africa, and Pakistan. But worse, there was no night life to speak of in Melbourne at all. The handsome, formal, leafy city shut down primly at dusk, even the pubs closing at 6 p.m. Ava felt she had wandered into some remote outpost, which apparently occasioned her much quoted remark to a reporter: "This is a picture about the end of the world. And it's just the place to make it."

In Melbourne, United Artists had taken over and converted an annex building of the St. James Hotel, in the suburb of South Yarra, for her and her entourage. That first evening, a cocktail reception had been arranged for her at the Savoy Plaza Hotel. Local "society" turned up in full force, but Ava at the last minute refused to come: she dreaded boring social events, and used the excuse that she didn't want to be tired for the next day's rehearsals. Instead, she went with Bappie to Antonio's, a small and excellent restaurant in the suburb of Toorak, where she ran into the English actor John McCallum and his wife, Googie Withers.

After rehearsals the next day, Ava accepted an invitation from the Australian tennis star Tony Trabert, whom she had met on the plane from San Francisco, to attend a match he was playing at the Velodrome against Merv Rose. When, after Trabert's victory, she and Tony left the match together in the Rolls Bentley which United Artists had hired, the press immediately jumped to the conclusion they were having an affair. Nothing could have been further from the truth: Ava was awaiting Walter hourly, and Trabert was very much married.

Aside from this minor gossip, it seemed that Ava's

Australian visit would be less marked by disastrous publicity than had her European appearances. But this was
not so. Her serious attempts to like the country were
short-lived.

I discussed the making of the picture with Tony Perkins in 1970 in his trailer at Paramount where he was
making a TV horror show called *How Awful About
Allan*. As spidery and angular as ever, with the broad,
shallow chest and narrow waist of an Egyptian carving,
he was excessively nervous, his head twisting to and fro as
though he were bound hand and foot in a chair. "It was a
miserable picture to make," he said. "But not because of
Ava. She tried very hard, she was courageous, but the
environment was completely impossible for her. She was
used to a sophisticated night life and Melbourne had
none. She was used to being pampered by men, but
Australian men were rough-and-ready and had no idea
how to treat a woman. Kramer drove her very hard. She
worked like a Trojan: up on the set early, seldom rested,
studied her lines with desperate intensity, took any punishment the picture handed her without complaint. But
all the time, in every moment of every scene, I knew she
wanted the hell out of there. She wanted to go home."

Kramer said: "She could be the warmest person in the
world. One day after shooting we went to an Australian
submarine and she talked to a sailor about his life in a
small town. Then suddenly she was bored, and he was
bewildered. She can be warm and sweet and then suddenly cut it all off. When we filmed the last love scene
between Ava and Peck she asked for just three minutes to
think. She walked to the end of a pier, stared into the
water, and came back to portray an emotional breakdown. Later, I told her to jump in the water for a shot.
She did, cold and filthy though it was. Often she'd play
several sets of tennis before the day's work, then suddenly

look bored. When that happened at the beginning of a day's shooting, look out! But most of the time she was just acting bored! For two-thirds of the picture she stopped drinking. Then she started again."

Fred Astaire, delicate and fastidious in his elegant white house in Beverly Hills, had only the warmest memories of both the picture and Ava: "I loved every moment of *On the Beach*," he said. "First of all, I was playing a scientist, which was a very welcome change of pace. Second, I thought Ava absolutely lovable and adorable. It's true she was a little, shall I say, *flustered* at times on the set. But she never let it show in her playing, as I think anyone who saw the picture would agree. If there was a tragic undercurrent in the humor of her playing, then that was entirely appropriate to the tragic *subject* of the picture itself. I was staying in the great mansion of a formidable Australian woman, Dame Mabel Brookes. I often used to have Ava over and she would chuckle delightedly over the ornate Victorian decor. She was a *love!*"

Ava's first sequence, in which she held Gregory Peck in a passionate embrace, was shot in temperatures of 109 degrees. On the sand of Canadian Bay, 30 miles from Melbourne, under the hot arc lights, the temperature was 130 degrees, and between shots makeup people had to reconstruct Ava's sweat-streaked face 19 times. Back at her hotel suite exhausted each night, with nowhere to go except Antonio's, she fretted miserably. She could not sleep, and in desperation sent for Walter to come to her at once. In the meantime, Tony Trabert continued to invite her to tennis matches.

On January 18, Walter arrived, looking pale and exhausted, and almost from the beginning Ava picked quarrels with him. On edge because of the heat, the flies, and

the boredom of her environment, she made him as always
the scapegoat, a role he bore with almost saintly tolerance
and good humor until, by early February, it became obvious to him that Ava's romantic interest in him, such as it
was, had completely burned out.

As though wanting to announce the fact publicly,
Walter was seen with an attractive girl, Dawn Kellar,
who performed an amateurish belly dance at a show he
gave at the Sydney Stadium. Ava flew up for Walter's
Saturday night performance, but the next day she was
barely talking to him. She flew back to Melbourne, and
gave an extraordinary party, possibly the most extrava-
gant in Melbourne up to that time, which culminated in
two of the guests dragging a pair of horses up the stairs,
where the guests gave the horses glasses of champagne.

Ava underwent a widely publicized ordeal when for a
particular scene she had to be tossed overboard from a
boat at Frankston Beach. Photographers were forbidden
to come near the shooting, as she was ducked six times
and emerged dripping wet under Stanley Kramer's careful
instructions. But they took the photographs of her sodden
face and figure with telephoto lenses anyway.

Sinatra arrived in Melbourne the first week of February to give two concerts for promoter Lee Gordon. He
had agreed to do them for Ava's sake: she had become
eager to see him to break the monotony of Australian
life. Terrified of the publicity which would attend her
meeting him at the airport, she turned up unexpectedly at
his second concert at the Melbourne Stadium. But the
press bore down on them as she left the stadium in
Frank's limousine, and she had to make a rapid getaway.
As a result, she barely saw him at all. He left the next day
for concerts in Sydney.

As the shooting wore on, Ava became increasingly restless and anxious to return to Madrid. Her only consola-

tions were Stanley Kramer's calm and considerate handling of her, her great liking and admiration for Fred
Astaire and the Gregory Pecks, and her personal helpers
on the set: the ever reliable Mearene, the English makeup
man John O'Gorman, and her kindly wardrobe assistant,
Eva Friend. But she could even be impossible with her
own circle. Ruth Waterbury, who covered the picture,
recalls: "One night Gregory and Veronique Peck invited
Ava to dinner, and she sat outside the dinner party all
evening in the hall, refusing to speak to anyone and embarrassing her host and hostess."

Stanley Kramer says: "Ava was marvelous once she
got going, got rid of that small pressing inhibition she had
that she was no good. She worked ferociously, she believed in her part, but she was terribly distracted by the
eagerness of the spectators to see her in every scene on
every location, and by the relentlessness of the Australian
press, which was so starved of local news."

At weekends, or in rare breaks in shooting, Ava fled
the confines of Melbourne for the more raffish attractions
of Sydney. Unlike Melbourne, Sydney was sensual, ap-
pealingly seedy, and full of physically attractive, noisy,
and energetic people. In 1959, Sydney was a shabby
urban mess. But at least it had a rudimentary night life in
the area known as Kings Cross, a crowded, Soho-like
district filled with tiny cafes, spectacularly littered sidewalks, and a variety of dives reminiscent of Rome's. The
horrors were real enough—cockroaches carpeted the
sidewalks under the neon glare at night and flies penetrated even the most expensive bars—but in all its garish
squalor Kings Cross symbolized life.

The trouble was that Sydney had one of the most efficient and brashest press corps in the world, as tough as
any in Europe or the United States in its pursuit of news.
Despite the fact that Ava used the name of "Miss Gor-

don" for her first week-long trip on February 8, and checked into the Hotel Buckingham at Point Piper, overlooking Sydney Harbor, under that name, the press found her out and pursued her to dinner at the harborside Caprice Restaurant where she had gone with Tony Trabert and Bappie at the invitation of the American owner. She left the restaurant at 12:45 a.m., and checked out of the Buckingham, moving into another hotel half an hour later. But still the reporters followed her.

The same week she was having a drink at the Corinthian Room Club after visits to Romano's and Andre's nightclubs when a group of photographers took pictures of her with friends. She tolerated these but refused to sign the Corinthian Room autograph book—the first time this had happened in the history of the club. An Australian Navy petty officer came nervously to her table and asked her to sign his autograph book, to which she agreed. Just as she had finished signing, a young reporter from the *Sydney Sun* came to her table and began attempting an impromptu interview. Her nerves already stretched to the limit, Ava was infuriated by this latest example of local brashness. She picked up her champagne glass and hurled it at him so that it shattered against his chest. Next morning Ava flew back to Melbourne to report for shooting, only to read a headline: "AVA BUBBLES OVER!"

By mid-February, the shooting of *On the Beach* barely done, Ava flew to California without giving a final press conference.

Back in San Francisco, Ava turned down a suggestion she should go to Hollywood for promotions on *The Naked Maja*, and instead flew to Haiti. In June, Ava was in Florida, trying to reach Sinatra without success in his various haunts there. She moved about constantly for the next six months, from New York to Palm Springs to

Mexico, battling with airline officials who refused to admit her corgis to a plane, and with traffic police who arrested her for speeding and holding an expired driver's license.

In Madrid, she rested for several weeks, exhausted. At La Bruja with her beloved corgis, she steadily pulled herself back to the life she had enjoyed before she left, encouraged by the excellent preview responses to the first screenings of *On the Beach*.

Ava flew to New York in the fall of 1959, where Frank had arranged to give her the use of an apartment. This was to be only one of countless acts of generosity to her in the years that followed. She in her turn was deeply loyal to him, and to her other husbands, frequently assisting Mickey Rooney during the dark days of his career in the 1960s, and always speaking warmly of Artie Shaw in the period in which he lived in Spain.

It was while she was staying in New York that Ava had a telephone call from an old friend, Nunnally Johnson. He told her he had been asked to write the screenplay for, and to direct, a novel by Bruce Marshall, *The Fair Bride*, an intriguing story set in Spain during the Spanish Civil War, and he wanted her for the role of a prostitute who was in love with an embittered priest.

Ava was intrigued by the story, and by the fact that she could make it in Madrid. But again to her annoyance the Spanish government refused to allow the film to be made in Spain, forcing the company to transfer to the Titanus Studios in Rome.

The Fair Bride, retitled *The Angel Wore Red*, began shooting in Rome on November 2, 1959. An earlier plan to have Sinatra play the priest fell through, and Dirk Bogarde was cast instead. But anxious though Ava was to play the role well for Johnson, it was obvious to him that she had lost a great deal of composure and personal discipline.

Nunnally Johnson spoke to me 14 years later in his mansion in Beverly Hills. Tired, and seriously ill with emphysema, he had been ordered by his doctors to have absolute rest, but he agreed to see me in the afternoon of a summer's day. He was surrounded by a babble of people who were marching all over his expensive rugs, discussing the value of everything: his mansion was up for sale. He looked pale, his eyes a watery gray-blue. But his intelligence was as finely honed as ever.

"I adored Ava," Johnson said, "but she was a real headache for a production company. She traveled with 30 pieces of luggage, all of which had to go with the plane as she was terrified of losing it. She was a sultana in terms of her accommodations, the accoutrements of a star. She had a succession of secretaries who collapsed under the strain of handling all of these things. Sometimes a man, sometimes a woman. They couldn't take the pace. She had to be escorted to nightclubs, she couldn't go alone. She'd stay up all night. Even when we shot in Sicily she found all-night places, and that's like finding all-night places in Alabama.

"Sometimes she would do a scene particularly well. I would thank her and she would fall in my arms and say, 'Christ, you *know* I can't act.' And I'd say, 'What is it then? It's just as good as acting.' But she never believed me.

"She was a hillbilly girl who was going through a role she couldn't sustain in life. I told her, 'You can't be a Southerner because you aren't called Ava Jean.' Everyone in the South is an Ava Jean or a Mary Jean. Well, she found out I had a middle name, Nunnally Hunter. So at the end of each day in a very Southern accent she'd say, 'Nunnally Hunter. Five o'clock! Time for a little booze,

don't you think?' And I'd say, equally 'Deep South,' 'Ava
Jean, you're certainly owright, honey.' I tell you this.
That woman can handle more booze than any woman or
man I know. She'd drink for 24 hours at a stretch. And
then she'd come on the set, letter-perfect—well, more or
less.

"I think she first tasted moonshine when she was a kid.
She liked to drink early in the day. She'd say, 'Do you
like *grappa*?' That's the cheapest kind of Italian wine. I
said 'No.' She'd insist I taste it. I did, and I said, 'Moonshine!' And she said, 'I thought you'd recognize it!'

"At times she would get difficult, impossible. We were
shooting one night outside of Rome. I had just one more
shot of her to take. The assistant came to me and said,
'Miss Gardner says she won't finish the scene.' I went
over to her trailer and she was sitting there with some of
her friends. She said, 'I'm pissed off with this whole picture.' I said, 'Look, Ava, there's only one more shot. Do
it, otherwise the whole unit will have to come back here.'
That didn't stir her at all. She didn't care, and she
wouldn't do it. So we had to come back all that way, just
for her. The Italian people said to me, 'What would happen if something like this occurred in Hollywood?' I said,
'I'd simply pack up and go home to bed.' And that's
exactly what I did.

"On another occasion we had to film the interior of a
bombed-out church. It was a special set. She had to come
through a door followed by Dirk. I needed a special setup
to cover this. She was supposed to be on the set at seven
but by ten she hadn't shown up. I said to the cameraman,
'Hell, if she isn't here, let's shoot Dirk anyway.' Well,
Jesus Christ, if she doesn't arrive just while we're shooting Dirk. She blew her stack, got in her car, and went
home. The Italian assistants were horrified, but I took it
all in my stride.

"Ava is like Marilyn," Nunnally Johnson says. "She's really frightened. She would cry a lot, she had no confidence in herself, she felt she couldn't act, she had no home, no base, no family, she missed them terribly, she felt she'd missed out in life. It was hard to believe her unhappiness. When you looked at her, even then, she was—as Alistair Cooke always said—the most beautiful human being in the world.

"And yet she was obsessed with the injury to her face. She talked about it eternally. I couldn't see the god-damned thing. She'd go to the makeup man, she'd go back and look in the mirror, she was certain everybody could see it, but it was totally invisible. She often would say, 'All I have is my beauty. If that goes, there's nothing left.'

"She was constantly mooning about her lack of any family life. I remember one day she read that Olivia de Havilland had had a baby at the age of 41. Ava was about 37 at the time. She said, 'Well, I've got four years, anyway. I'm so miserable I haven't been a mother.' I told her, 'Well, for somebody that wants the vine-covered cottage and all of that, you certainly picked one hell of a parlay. Mickey Rooney, Artie Shaw, Frank Sinatra! What the hell made you expect to get anything out of that!' She didn't have a reply."

One of the few pleasant memories Johnson has of *The Angel Wore Red* is that Bappie flew in for Christmas and cooked a traditional Southern meal which, he says, "is the most delicious thing I have ever eaten."

While Ava was shooting in Rome, *On the Beach* was successfully released in December 1959, and earned her some of the best press notices of her career. Several critics cruelly pointed out that her role as a heavy-drinking party girl was a case of "type casting," a statement that caused her anguish or amusement, according to which mood she was in and which friends she happened to be with. But generally the reviews were strong, even though *Newsweek*'s review must have given her pause: "Miss Gardner has never looked worse or been more effective."

Bosley Crowther called the film an important and moving work, and at last gave Ava credit for her playing: "Surprisingly good, beyond conformance, are Fred Astaire in the straight serious role of the scientist and Ava Gardner as the worldly woman who finds serenity in love."

Chapter 13

THE MOVIE *The Angel Wore Red* was so disastrous it was barely released in the United States and had only sporadic showings in Europe. Ava was disappointed: despite her behavior, she had worked very hard on her role. She withdrew from picture-making for two years. Bored, she spent much of her time at La Bruja playing records, and seldom went out; finally, she became irritated with the house, and in 1961 she sold it, moving into the Hotel Richmond on a corner of the Plaza de la Republica Argentina in the noisy heart of Madrid. She told a friend who visited her there, "They leave me alone here. I've been around so long, people take me for granted." From the hotel, she spent months supervising work on a new top floor duplex apartment she had obtained at 8 Calle Dr. Arce, decorating it herself and moving in some of the furniture she had used at La Bruja.

The apartment was above the one where Peron, the exiled dictator of Argentina lived with his wife. The district was so filled with Americans it was known bitterly as "Korea" at the time. Her parties, flamenco dancing, and guitar playing with her friends aggravated the Perons beyond endurance. So much so that they called the police one night. When the police arrived, Ava asked them in for a drink. The officers accepted and left smiling sheepishly.

These parties, made up of a motley group of largely homosexual friends, movie buffs, scholars, hangers-on, and bullfight aficionados, were few and far between, and even quite decorous. Despite much Madrid talk of "round beds" or "daisy chains," the probability is that Ava slept entirely alone after these parties. A characteristic sight, as her former press agent David Hanna later noted, was "Ava in the early hours of the morning, rounding the Plaza de la Republica Argentina, with two barking corgis straining at the leash."

Ava endured yet another vicious smear from *Confidential*, accusing her of having numerous affairs with bullfighters. These charges were as false and absurd as those which had her sexually allied with Sammy Davis, Jr. Aside from Cabre and Dominguin, she had enjoyed brief affairs with only two bullfighters: Curro Girón, a fine artist in the ring; and a second-rate performer, Cumillano; neither of these was of more than a passing concern to her.

A pleasant interlude during this period was a visit from an old friend, Alana, the young and pretty daughter of Alan Ladd. Ava cut out drinking and devoted herself to being a mother to the girl. During Alana's stay, Sinatra sent word he was coming to visit Madrid. Ava worked desperately hard on the apartment, cleaning and dusting to the point of exhaustion so that it would be comfortable for his stay. But when he arrived he declined to stay with her, and left town very quickly; she was so bitterly upset she burst into tears.

Ava's behavior became more and more erratic. She invited several people to dinner and then failed to turn up. She gave a large party and when the guests arrived she was fast asleep in bed. Her peculiar behavior caused her to be crucified by the pitiless Italian journalist Oriana Fallaci. Signora Fallaci, with her friend Lucia Bose Dominguin, had, after weeks of negotiation with Ava's secretary, secured an appointment for an interview at 8 Calle Dr. Arce. When she arrived, she waited for hours, only to be informed that Ava "had a painful shoulder and was being massaged."

Ava then promised to call Oriana Fallaci in the evening and make another appointment. She did not call. Nor did she the next morning, afternoon, or evening. Oriana Fallaci, knowing Ava's terror of recording her voice on tape, wrote: "No doubt Ava dreamed of ever-turning ribbons of tape that twisted and strangled her as they wound about her neck."

At last a letter arrived, typed on blue stationery and signed by Ava herself, summoning her to come over with Lucia the following evening at nine. The note continued: "For a drink, not for an interview. I can't imagine why anybody would want to have an interview with me. I'm such a dull subject."

The following night, Oriana and Lucia Bose arrived at the apartment, to a loud burst of Spanish music and a clashing of glassware. The door opened slowly, and a face peeped out; Fallaci described Ava's eyes as large, frightened, hard with suspicion, underslung by bluish bags of flesh. Fallaci relentlessly noted the (almost invisible) mark of Ava's scar, and told her readers later that Ava's cheeks were "asymmetrical." "Her real wounds are her eyes," Oriana wrote in Italian. "Her breasts, in a red-flowered cheong-san, assail you arrogantly, all this maternal abundance corrected by two muscular and highly nervous arms. She shook my hand without warmth and without seeking my eyes."

Inside, Ava introduced Oriana and Lucia to an airline pilot, her secretary Ed Schaefer, and Bappie's husband. Ava said, "I'm terrified of microphones." Oriana assured her that there would be none. Ava told her she hated America, and would soon quit Spain for good. She would live in England: "I have always loved England. Or should I say, I have always loved to travel, to be a displaced person. I don't like to stay too long in the same place. I'm a gypsy, two suitcases and a ticket and I'm content. There are many places I could have lived. Italy. But those damned *paparazzi*! And then there is Honolulu: but they won't leave me alone there either. And Japan, I love Japan. But it seems there isn't a place on the globe where I can walk without being photographed, interviewed. . . . I hope you aren't interviewing me now! And then there is London. London, they take three or four photographs when you arrive and then they forget you exist. I love London, the climate, the people."

Fallaci said: "But there is no sun in London. It rains all the time."

Ava replied: "What does the sun mean to me? I never see the sun. I sleep during daylight. The night is company. It clarifies my mind. When I was a child, I was terrified of the dark. I cried all the time. Not now. I love the rain in London. The thin, fine rain . . . it gives me tranquility for a time. It appeases me."

Shortly after this visit, Ava endured the shocking news of the suicide of Ernest Hemingway. She had seen him recently in cities on both sides of the Atlantic. Now she learned in Madrid that on July 2 at his home in Ketchum, Idaho, after a trip to the Mayo Clinic and two attempts to jump off a plane, he had shot himself through the head, following his father into suicide.

In the winter of 1962, Ava was back in New York, visiting the latest nightspots. Columnists' legmen followed her: to the Chateau Madrid—she fled angrily when a flamenco dancer named Raoul took pictures of her; to the home of Guy Pastor, to see his famous father, Tony Pastor; to Count Basie's at Birdland; and back to the Chateau Madrid, all in the same night, to dance with the conductor Pupi Campo. *Photoplay* recorded: "She brought four—some say five—men to a party given by fashion photographer Bill Helburn. One of her escorts stood on his head in the middle of the floor to amuse her, but she was only bored. One afternoon she went to Freedomland —she was like a kid—went on all the rides, stuffed herself on hot dogs and candy, vowed she'd come back soon. . . . Late at night she sat in the Absinthe House eating a sirloin steak. She poured her own special sauce on the meat— heated champagne."

She described a curious little incident in New York to a writer for the *Ladies' Home Journal*: "It was after a party. I couldn't find a cab to take me back to my hotel. I was standing there on the street, at four in the morning, when along came a garbage truck. Two men called out, 'Hey, Ava, want a lift?' 'Sure do,' I said. And they hoisted me up and drove me back to the hotel. I invited them up to my suite for a few drinks. Fifteen minutes later, the night manager called up and said, 'Miss Gardner, I wonder if you'd mind asking your friends to move their, uh, vehicle from the front entrance!'"

* * *

Walter Chiari was in New York appearing in a play called *The Gay Life*, and he was frequently seen after the show with Ava at Basin Street East, the Copacabana, the Stork Club, and "21." Her name was also linked romantically with the baseball star Roger Maris—a publicity stunt, as it turned out.

Most of 1962 was spent doing virtually nothing: living quietly at the apartment in Madrid, entertaining some of her circle, keeping in touch with American friends like Sidney Guilaroff and Cukor, often seeing the Dominguins and the decorator Harris Williams, and very occasionally running for friends a 16mm print of some film she had starred in, from her collection of her own pictures, accompanied by ribald comments about her acting and appearance.

A friend, Betty Wallers, described her at the time: "Dinner parties Ava gave often stretched to 24 or even 36 hour parties and men used to drop exhausted like soldiers on a forced march. When her escorts were as limp as spaghetti, Ava would fling off her shoes and do a flamenco dance. . . . She would call me at 3 a.m. and ask me to 'a marvelous party.' She would introduce me to a 'great flamenco singer' and it would turn out to be the elevator boy.

"One night she took off to London and we went to Covent Garden together. Later, we went to a nightclub. She was wearing a white chiffon gown, diamonds, and a tiara. She swept into the ladies' room. The moment we got inside, Ava lifted her dress and wriggled her girdle off. After more contortions she got off her undies. Then she took off the tiara and the diamond bracelets. The whole lot was stuffed in our handbags. 'Thank goodness I am me again!' Ava shouted. And wriggling happily, with nothing on under her dress, she went back into the club.

And later on she took the entire band home with her when the club closed."

According to Betty Wallers: "Coming home, whether in London or Madrid, she always changed into sweaters and jeans. One night her maid, who had been working for days without sleep, went berserk. She ran into the kitchen and emerged with two carving knives. As she went for Ava I grabbed her, slapped her, and she dropped the knives."

Ava told the *Ladies' Home Journal* at the time: "Being a film star is still a big damn bore. I do it for the money, that's all. After all these years I don't know a damn thing about movies. I was put under contract when I was 18 because I was pretty, and since I made my first picture I haven't done a damn thing that's worthwhile. I was never an actress. As a girl I was thrown out of high school plays. I've often tried to give it up. But I've got to do something and I don't know how to do anything else. I can't write, or paint, or anything. I did once think of becoming a nurse. But I know I'd vomit every time a patient vomited. I wouldn't be much use. I could be a secretary again, I suppose. . . . If I had more drive, more interest, maybe I'd have done better; I don't know. As it is I never know what's going on. I had dinner with George Cukor not long ago, and he and his friends were going on about the business and what was happening and do you know I didn't understand a damn thing they were talking about. As for acting, I know nothing about it."

She became more and more simple in her style of dress: a dressing gown did service for days on end, or she wore knit pullovers, sweaters, cardigans, with English pleated skirts and jersey jackets, all tasteful and unpretentious. In the earlier days in Spain, she had sought to create an impression with dresses by Valentino, Dior, and Schubert, but now she preferred the less ostentatious style of the Spanish designer Pedro Rodriguez, splurging only on one birthday, when she bought a fantastic Balenciaga creation. She had always disliked heavy jewelry, and seldom wore it. Most of her time was spent at home, and she almost never gave the sort of parties with which her name had become associated, particularly in Mexico. She spent little, though she gave a monthly allowance to Mickey Rooney when he was broke, virtually maintained Bappie, and always sent gifts to friends in need: when a homosexual in her circle expressed admiration for a bolero jacket she was wearing, she gave it to him at once.

During 1962, plans were going ahead in Madrid for a large, dumb epic called *Fifty-five Days at Peking*. Philip Yordan, who had started Ava's career as a serious actress, had become a resident of Spain; he ran into Ava very occasionally at restaurants or at parties, talking to her briefly—no more impressed with her than he had been some 17 years before. He began writing a script for Samuel Bronston, whose story department he headed. It was based on an idea which had been considered by Jerry Wald at 20th Century-Fox and discarded: the story of the Boxer Rebellion in China, the defense of the city of Peking by representatives of a dozen nations under the guidance of the British ambassador to the court of the Dowager Empress Tzu-Hsi. Yordan saw the subject as ideal for the international market, for it would appeal to many people and have an uplifting democratic message. He and Bronston cast Charlton Heston as a strong and authoritative American major who solves some serious problems; David Niven as a coolly efficient British envoy; Dame Flora Robson as the Dowager Empress. Then he offered Ava the important role of a Russian countess married to Niven.

Although she thought the script ridiculous, she accepted the part in order to bolster her sagging finances.

From the outset, the production was a disaster. Because of his failing financial position, Bronston had to fake the appearance of a great epic; he used sets from his *Decline and Fall of the Roman Empire*, crudely converted into a simulacrum of 19th century Peking, the Peking Temple created from the Roman Forum. The Crystal Palace of the Dowager Empress of China already stood in a park in Valencia.

The most difficult and expensive part of the operation was the staging of the action scenes. The director, Nicholas Ray, was drinking heavily. A special assistant, the veteran Andrew Marton, flew in to take over. Marton helped assemble about 3500 extras and 46 stunt men. Since there was not a sufficient number of Chinese available in Spain (only 307 could be conveniently found), 1500 were airlifted in from all parts of the world.

The location was known as Las Matas or "The Shrubs," a stretch of fields and low-lying scrub under the shadow of the Sierra de Guadarrama, some 17 miles northwest of Madrid.

Ava hated every moment of making the picture, especially the sequence in the Boxer Rebellion in which the Countess is almost trampled by the crowd. Ava drank testily in her dressing room before each take.

Charlton Heston, in a hotel room in Sydney, Australia, in 1965, spoke with disgust of the picture. His craggy face flushed with displeasure, his yoke-like shoulders shrugged with despair at the memory. "*Fifty-five Days at Peking* was one of the most disagreeable experiences of my entire life," he said, in a soft, discreet voice which was entirely at odds with his on-screen growl or his Monument Valley physique. "First of all, we had no script at all. The lines were made up from day to day. The only reason I did the thing at all was as a favor to Phil Yordan, who told me he had several kids to feed and no money. I shouldn't have listened to a word he said.

"As for Ava—well, I must be careful. But let's say she wasn't the most disciplined or dedicated actress I ever worked with. A lot of the time she wasn't available for scenes. I think she was scared to death of her part. I can't really blame her. None of us should have made that piece of crap in the first place."

Philip Yordan was less charitable. "Her manner had grown disdainful, bitter, superior, contemptuous. All through the picture she was constantly drunk," he said. "When I complained she ran to Bronston's house and said I was ill-treating her. She would remain in her dressing room, terrified by the thousands of extras, and her double appeared in endless over-the-shoulder shots. In many scenes when she was needed and when Heston, who never wanted to make the picture in the first place but did it as a favor to me, begged her to join him in a scene, she again hid, and drank, and sulked. The real reason was fear: she was terrified of the competition from the major British stars appearing in the film and terrified also of the mob. While Heston worked 16 hours a day, she did not, and I not only rewrote most of her scenes, I killed her off early in the picture. I found her snide, hard, corrupt, impossible, light-years removed from the simple befuddled girl I had known in the 1940s, and still as incapable of reading lines."

Top-heavy, grandiose, ridiculously overacted, *Fifty-five Days at Peking* helped to destroy Bronston's career, severely damaged Ava's, and virtually finished Nicholas Ray's. Neither a critical nor commercial success, it was survived only by David Niven and Charlton Heston, and it left nothing pleasant in Ava's memory except working

with Niven again. Her performance was among her worst
—actressy, coarse, clumsy.

Ava next accepted an invitation to go to Hollywood to
play a small but important part in John Frankenheimer's
film of *Seven Days in May*, the novel about a plot by the
military against the President of the United States. Ava
liked the script by Rod Serling. She was cast as the discarded mistress of General Scott (Burt Lancaster), a
martinet determined to make his way to the seat of government at the White House. She played her brief scenes
with extraordinary pathos, a sense of despair and sadness
which could not have been entirely assumed. Though
director Frankenheimer records that she was drinking
heavily and was not as punctual on the set as she had
once been, he found her extremely sensitive and responsive to the part, with which she clearly identified. She was
badly shocked though by what she felt was the rough
treatment given her by the cameraman, the expert Ells-
worth Fredericks. She looked drastically aged, with
pouches under her eyes, sunken cheeks, and sallow skin,
and in some shots she looked as though she had just been
crying.

In common with most of her pictures, this was an
unhappy one in terms of personal conflicts. Franken-
heimer says: "I had my problems with Ava, and also with
Kirk Douglas. He was jealous of Burt Lancaster. He felt
he was playing a secondary role to him. . . . I told him
before he went in, he would be. He wanted to be Burt
Lancaster. He's wanted to be Burt Lancaster all his life.
In the end it came to sitting down with Douglas, saying,
'Look, you prick, if you don't like it, get the hell out.'"
The film also caused a governmental conflict: President
John Kennedy wanted it made, and loaned the White

House for some scenes; the Pentagon did not, and fought the making of the picture.

It was completed in July 1963. The reviews were almost uniformly excellent. Ava's fine portrayal of breakdown and defeat earning her praise and confirming her belief that despite her problems with Frankenheimer she had made the right decision in appearing in this serious film. Her greatest gratification was in reading that Bosley Crowther, her bitter critic for many years, called her performance "superb," and ranked her alongside Lancaster and Kirk Douglas and Fredric March. In its attacks on incipient fascism in America she felt the film was important, and she was delighted that even her harshest critics felt the same.

Unhappily, the film had rather a shaky time at the box office, and it did little for Ava's career.

Chapter 14

I
N AUGUST 1963, AVA RECEIVED a transatlantic phone
call from her old friend, director John Huston,
whom she had first met and liked on the set of *The
Killers*. Tall and bony, with a long, horsy face and a
dangerous charm, he had many of the qualities—humor,
honesty, strength, creative energy—she admired in men.
With her uncanny instinct, she had recognized his bril-
liance and force of character from the first. Like Hemingway—but with far greater security in his masculinity, far
less need to prove himself—he had an enormous, envelop-
ing warmth and an ability to melt opposition that she
found irresistible.

Their friendship had remained profound despite their

infrequent meetings over the years. It was based on mutual regard, an intense empathy, a deep understanding of each other's strength, ruthlessness, sensitivity, and capacity to wound. There had never been a question of a love affair.

The long distance call at 8 Calle Dr. Arce was enormously welcome. In minutes, Ava was responding with roars of laughter to Huston's wit. When he told her he wanted to come to Madrid and talk to her about a new part, she accepted at once. But when he told her he wanted her to play Maxine, the hotel-keeper in Tennessee Williams' *Night of the Iguana*, she was terrified. She knew that Bette Davis had wanted the film role, had played the part brilliantly on the stage, and Ava dared not face that particular competition. Huston explained to her that the role was no longer that of a ravening monster "who ate her mate alive." He had made it more touching, accessible, and sympathetic. Huston pressed on, determined to overcome her fear.

I talked to John Huston in 1973 in his sprawling ranch-type house next to the Will Rogers State Memorial Park in Pacific Palisades, California. In an atmosphere of his own carvings and brilliantly vivid paintings and—outside the tall windows—racehorses and happily screaming children, he looked rather like a handsome old racehorse himself. Dressed in a shapeless boiler-suit, smoking a giant cigar, he loped about, in a crouching, thrusting movement, his voice crackling like parchment. The very mention of Ava's name sent him careening around the room excitedly; then he sprawled in a chair, put his enormous feet on a table, prodigally scattered ash about, and began to reminisce, savoring her name as though he were rolling a fine wine around on his tongue: "Ava! There was nobody in the world who could play Maxine. She was—is—a very fine actress, though she thinks she's lousy. I knew she had the kind of random gallant, wild openness Maxine had along with the 'other side' of Ava, which is very 'close,' and almost secretive," he says.

"I knew she was very doubtful whether she could do the part. I flew to Madrid to talk it over with her. After a great deal of persuasion she reluctantly agreed. But the moment she signed the contract all of her doubts re-emerged.

"It was a question of making her see that she should really do it. I think I told her that Tennessee Williams and I had quarreled over the writing of her part for the screen. I had told Williams, 'Tennessee, I think you have something in your craw about older women. You don't like them. You're trying to do something *perverse* with the part!' and Tennessee had smiled and said, 'Well, that's possible, John!' Ava and I laughed about that."

Despite Huston's charm, Ava remained terrified of the part. She simply didn't feel that she would be up to it, and both public and critics would laugh her off the screen. Huston went back to America and began preparing the picture, while she remained in Madrid. Even when she got word to come to Mexico—the setting of the picture—and start work she remained afraid. "I'm not an actress," she kept telling friends. "What does he want me for?" Only three or four days before shooting was to begin at Puerto Vallarta on the Mexican coast, Ava was fretting miserably at her suite in the Hotel Bamer in Mexico City.

"We had a difficult session," Huston recalls. "Her doubts were coming to the surface and overwhelming her. I had to be firm with her. I said, 'Come on, Ava, that's quite enough of this now, you're going to do it, you've got to do it, and I don't want to hear *one more word* about backing out of it.' Finally she shrugged and said, 'Well, all right.' And she *did* it!"

* * *

In late September 1963, Ava was due to have her first fittings with costume designer Dorothy Jeakins. According to Huston's assistant Thelda Victor, "Ava gave Dorothy Jeakins a bad time. She kept her waiting over an hour and a half while she played gin rummy with Sandy Whitelaw, assistant to the producer Ray Stark. Then, when she watched her costume tests in the projection room, she started to cry. Somebody told me it was because she looked so awful."

On September 29, Ava's trusted friend, Sidney Guilaroff, arrived to dress her hair, pulling it tightly back in a ponytail. More or less ready, Ava left for the location at Puerto Vallarta and Mismaloya, a small town on the Pacific coast of Mexico, on October 28, 1963.

The flight to Puerto Vallarta in an ancient DC-6 was a bumpy, dangerous nightmare all the way. On arrival, Ava found that Puerto Vallarta was completely cut off from the outside world—with temperamental electricity and no telephone or telegraph. With Mearene Jordan, an accountant, and her corgis, Ava installed herself in Puerto Vallarta and set up an air conditioner in a small rented house. "Look at it," she told writer Stephen Birmingham. "Look where they installed it! In the wall between the kitchen and the living room! It blows cold air in the kitchen and hot air in the living room."

In Mismaloya, the cast was assembled: Richard Burton, who played an unfrocked minister, Sue Lyon, who played an amorous schoolgirl, Deborah Kerr, the intellectual daughter of a poet played by Cyril Delevanti.

A stream of special correspondents and magazine and newspaper writers poured into Mismaloya to cover the shooting. Most made much of the complicated interrelationships of the cast: Peter Viertel, now married to Deborah Kerr, had been Ava's date for a time; John Huston's wife was Evelyn Keyes, who had once been married to

Artie Shaw; Elizabeth Taylor's ex-husband Michael Wilding was now her fiancé Richard Burton's agent; and so forth. Elizabeth Taylor was on the site simply as a visitor, but she had, according to Stephen Birmingham in *Cosmopolitan Magazine*, brought quite an entourage: two native maids, a laundress, a green parrot, and a former slot machine repairman whose job was to massage Burton's flabby stomach.

At Mismaloya, 283 natives and 90 burros had carved out a special village from the jungle, which was stiflingly hot and crawling with animal life and vermin. Spiders as large as hands crawled on the walls of the crude wooden huts; the air was filled with flies which clung stickily to the actors' faces; gnats and daddy longlegs constantly became entangled in the cast's hair. The only accessibility to Puerto Vallarta was by water; from a punt, passengers were transferred to a motor launch, and thence to a crude pier. Ava chose to go in on waterskis behind her own speedboat each day, making an exhilarating and cooling experience out of what might have been an insufferable ordeal.

For two days, drenching rain made shooting impossible. Columnists kept arriving on the scene, insisting that Ava talk about her "broken relationship" with Peter Viertel and her jealousy of Deborah Kerr, who was supposed to have taken Viertel from her. A flustered lady journalist, Helen Lawrenson, author of *Latins Are Lousy Lovers*, arrived, and got jumped on one night by Tennessee Williams' dog. Burton kept drinking tequila with beer chasers and Ava refused to have cameramen anywhere around her. Helen Lawrenson appeared to be watching Ava, who visibly resented her presence. Later, Miss Lawrenson wrote viciously about her in *Show Magazine*: ". . . She was her customary self, as amiable as an adder. . . . She gave [a photographer] a look Medusa might have envied. . . . Both Elizabeth Taylor and Ava are as spoiled as medieval queens. They expect men to fall at their feet, and they are accustomed to being catered to and having everything done for them. . . ."

In an attempt to avoid this kind of invasion of her privacy, Ava changed houses five times in Puerto Vallarta. Later, she lost her temper when *Life* photographer Gjon Mili took too many shots of her; she kicked him in the stomach and literally drove him off the set. She also fluffed a key line. In a scene in which she was shaving Burton as he lay in a hammock, she was supposed to say, "In a pig's eye you are!" Instead of which she said, "In a pig's ass!" and both she and Burton broke up laughing, accompanied by Huston and the crew.

She was terrified of a sequence in which she had to swim with two beach boys who were her lovers in the picture. John Huston made her join him in several stiff drinks and then he, almost naked, showed her exactly what he wanted her to do with the boys. "If I didn't know John better I'd have said he looked like a fairy," a bystander commented ironically. Ava almost played the part in actuality, swimming and waterskiing with a boy called Tony, but there was no romantic interest between them.

After several days of shooting, Huston gave each star in the cast—Richard Burton, Deborah Kerr, Sue Lyon, Ava—a gold-plated derringer with gold bullets, inscribed with the names of the others. "I told them they could always use the guns if the competition grew too fierce," he said. "I think on reflection I was lucky to have selected blanks!"

Deborah Kerr said later, "I sensed a certain nervousness in the laughter and thanks of everyone concerned. It was almost like the start of an Agatha Christie murder novel." Sometimes, Ava gave Deborah a lift in her speedboat, scotching rumors that she was fighting with her over Peter Viertel. Deborah was amazed by Ava's physical strength: not only waterskiing to work but frequently swimming out to the speedboat from the foreshores of Puerto Vallarta. "She has the strength of an ox, that girl!" Deborah said.

On the whole, Ava was punctual, although one morning she was so infuriated by a newspaper report that she was going to marry the Mexican film director Emilio Fernandez, who played a bartender in the picture, she held up shooting for hours while she fumed.

She protested loudly against shooting a scene in which she held a discussion with Deborah in a kitchen while Deborah cut the heads off fish: the smell appalled her, but under Huston's genially tough persuasion she managed to play the scene. It was a seemingly interminable sequence, and after numerous takes she broke down and forgot her lines.

Nevertheless, Ava adored John Huston throughout the shooting, and the feeling was mutual. She was very fond of Richard Burton's fiancée, Elizabeth Taylor, with whom she had much in common; she often told Liz jokingly, "Richard is the man *I* should have married. If you hadn't got him I certainly would have tried to get him. He's got a sense of humor and he's a *man*." She told a friend later, "Some people say Liz and I are whores, but we are saints; we do not hide our loves hypocritically, and when we love we are loyal and faithful to our men."

A red-faced and sweating Richard Burton, after a crowded press conference following a screening of *The Sandpiper* in 1965, told me about Ava in the picture. "She was wonderful," he said. "It's true she was terrified of playing the part of Maxine, as she felt she was entirely unsuited to it. But once she got into it her fantastic intuition took over. It was a question of empathy. She really *knew* that sad, defeated woman at 'the end of the world,' as it were, and at the end of her tether. Like Maxine, Ava was what they used to call in mystery thrillers 'a woman with a past.' "

On November 17, a distressing accident occurred: two assistant directors, Tom Shaw and Terry Morse, were sitting on a balcony of a cottage when the rotted wood beneath them gave way and sent them hurtling onto the ground. They both were in agony and had to be carried down the hill to a boat to be transferred to the hospital in Puerto Vallarta. Deborah Kerr wrote in her diary: "Night work is tough enough and it is tougher still without sleep. We didn't get to bed until 6 a.m. and I couldn't get to sleep at all. I kept seeing them both fall like ragdolls again and again all night long, and hearing Tom's terrible groans. . . ."

Another severe blow to everyone came on November 22, when news of the assassination of President Kennedy was broadcast. Ava was sitting in the Mismaloya bar drinking at 4:30 in the afternoon, in a state of shock, when a silently weeping Deborah Kerr joined her. Huston solemnly announced that shooting would continue, but when the assistant director Jaime Contreras called for a minute's silence during the early evening shooting, Ava and Deborah clung together and cried unashamedly.

The grief the news caused Ava, the stream of stories in the press creating wholly imaginary rivalries between her and others in the cast, weighed her down in the last weeks of shooting, and she did not even attend the cast and crew Thanksgiving Day party. Clearly, she felt, after Kennedy's death, there was nothing to have a Thanksgiving for, though she did go to the end-of-shooting party. Moody and depressed, she flew back to Mexico City, and thence to Madrid, just in time for Christmas and her forty-first birthday.

* * *

On July 7, 1964, Ava went to the premiere of *Night of the Iguana* in New York. A black tie audience paid $100 a seat to attend the opening at the Philharmonic Hall; the screening was followed by a champagne party and a banquet held on the second floor balcony. It was a squealing, shouting confusion of TV crews, reporters, and fans. When Richard Burton arrived after playing in *Hamlet* the shouts and screams became overpowering. Ava, in a pale blue strapless gown and a white lace greatcoat, had the lion's share of the photographs.

The reviews were excellent. Edith Oliver in *The New Yorker* rightly said that Ava was "absolutely splendid" as Maxine; Richard Cullahan in *Life* said her performance was the "revelation" of the picture and added, ". . . She can act. She does. And she all but runs away with the picture." *Newsweek* noted that Ava had reverted to her North Carolina drawl and said, "Her vowels are windblown, like her hair, and she is all high blood and blowziness . . . a great woman to play a great woman."

Chapter 15

FREQUENTLY, DURING THE mid-1960s, Ava would fly to London to see her great friend the conductor Sir Malcolm Sargent, who always arranged for a box to be reserved for her at Albert Hall or Festival Hall. Other friends she saw regularly in London, Rome, or Madrid were Noël Coward and Tennessee Williams. But most of the time, she preferred the company of her dearest friend Betty (Mrs. Richard) Sicre, who was the confidante Ruth Rosenthal and Frances Heflin had been in Hollywood days.

A writer for *Redbook Magazine* described Ava in this period: "[She is] haughty and demanding, playing flamenco records endlessly, marshalling her forces—her secretaries, drivers, maids, wardrobe women—to perform all the tasks that need to be done every day—dashing back to the apartment for some forgotten handkerchief, picking up champagne, buying the English newspapers, looking for a misplaced telephone number. She will quibble over a small bill, count the eggs in the cupboard, check over her silver for fear a gypsy visitor had stolen it. But she will cheerfully pay for a servant's operation or buy her sister a new car and go to great lengths to sneak it into the garage for Christmas Eve—wrapped in cellophane." She told *Redbook* in a rare interview: "I haven't taken an overdose of sleeping pills and called my agent. I haven't been in jail, and I don't go running to a psychiatrist every two minutes. That's something of an accomplishment these days."

In 1966, Ava, tired of the apartment at Calle Dr. Arce, moved to a rented chalet in an area known as the Colonia Ramira de Maetzu. Disliking it after a few months, she moved yet again—to a suite at the Castellana Hilton, which at least had the benefit of convenience.

Stories about her—apocryphal or not—were legion in Madrid at the time. A young flamenco dancer was supposed to have flung himself from a window because of his unrequited love for her. She was supposed to have been seen one evening in the Plaza Argentina dressed only in a bra and panties. There was a story that she had ruined a boyfriend's sports car with a monkey wrench after a quarrel. She was said to have invaded the switchboard of the Castellana Hilton yelling "Fire! Fire!" in the middle of the night, and even to have squatted down and defecated in the ornate lobby. She was reported to have smashed photographers' cameras, attacked a girl in a nightclub with a broken bottle, and entertained bellhops who brought her breakfast in bed. All of these scurrilous stories distressed her acutely.

Confidential Magazine summed up the world's image of her at the time: "Two o'clock in the morning. A gray Cadillac convertible races over the La Coruna highway north of Madrid. The driver is a woman whose auburn-red hair flies in the dry, warm wind. Next to her sits a beautiful young Spaniard with broad shoulders and narrow hips."

It was in this period that John Huston offered her the role of Sarah, barren wife to George C. Scott's Abraham in *The Bible*. The film was to be an enormously elaborate re-creation of several books of the Old Testament, and to be shot in various countries. In Rome, a great replica of Noah's Ark was to be built, and several scenes were to be shot in Israel and Egypt on the sites of the actual events.

Normally, Ava had a horror of epic films, and she was still recovering from the depressing experience of *Fifty-five Days at Peking*, but she accepted.

Once again, Huston had to coax Ava bit by bit into playing the part, showing her the beauty, suffering, and patience in the character of Sarah, the quiet acceptance with which she endured her barrenness, and the sweetness with which she made Abraham take another woman in order to sire a son. For Ava, who had never borne a child, the role evidently had a deep meaning, and although she later told Rex Reed she despised the role, she in fact studied it with fierce intensity, guided in the interpretation of every line by Huston.

The film was shot in mid-1964 at the De Laurentiis Studios, in various parts of Egypt and North Africa, as well as in Italy itself. It was on the whole a tolerable, even enjoyable experience for Ava, partly because of her belief in the role, chiefly because of the consideration and intelligence of Huston, whom more than ever she regarded as the one man alive she could wholly trust. Their friendship was certainly the most remarkable of her

career. The fascination was mutual: Huston still thinks of
her as one of the great women of the century; she thinks
of him as the only great director with whom she has
worked.

The only bone of contention in the making of the film,
and afterward, was George C. Scott. A brilliant actor,
who flung himself into the part of Abraham with absolute
devotion, Scott apparently became confused between life
and the screen, and began to see himself in the role of
Ava's husband. Fred Sidewater, Dino De Laurentiis' assistant, says: "Scott was crazy about her from the beginning, and I mean crazy. He even created a scene in a bar
when she was drinking quite harmlessly with Peter
O'Toole. He was hopelessly in love with her, and she was
not in love with him."

Sidewater surprised me by adding: "I had a taste of Ava
myself. One day I took some papers to her tent in the
Abruzzi for her to sign. She said, 'Oh, let's go to bed now
and I'll sign the papers later.' So we did, she signed the
papers, and I left."

The press doggedly followed the scenes of jealousy and
passion that made Scott pursue the reluctant Ava after
the picture was finished. According to several newspapers
he followed her from Rome to London, stormed into her
suite at the Savoy, threw her agent out of her suite, and
seized her violently.

"She literally fled from the hotel," Nunnally Johnson
says. "She hid in the servants' quarters which were cut off
from the rest of the hotel. Her agent was to take her to
the plane next morning. He said he was afraid she
wouldn't make it, she was so shattered by her experience
with Scott. She was disheveled, she looked terrible, and
he was terrified she wouldn't be able to get back into her
suite to pack. Next morning, the agent called her at the
Savoy and couldn't get her. The servants' quarters were

searched—no Ava. He decided he'd have to be brave and go to her suite, where Scott might be lurking. He arrived at her suite and a maid showed him in. After a while, Ava came in, and she looked glorious, as though nothing at all had happened."

John Huston says: "He was out of his mind over her—literally, and you can quote me. I have the greatest admiration for him as an actor and the greatest contempt for him as a man. Not only did he attack her at the Savoy—my understanding is he broke the door down—but he struck her and damn near broke her jaw. She was black and blue. She was so terrorized she was hysterical. He began chasing her clear across the map—he even made a terrible scene after he had followed her to Hollywood and traced her down to the Beverly Hills Hotel. When he found she was there he went up to her room and kicked the door down and molested her. At one stage in all of this he had to be put away in a nursing home. That's what love did to the man."

In 1965, Ava got a call from her old friend Vincent Sherman, who had directed her in *Lone Star*. He wanted her to play an "expensive kept woman" in a version of the life of Cervantes. With Harry Weinstein, the producer, and David Karp, the writer, Sherman visited her in Madrid and talked to her for an hour and a half.

Ava didn't warm to Weinstein and after a few yawns and a few drinks said, "Vince and I know each other from way back. Why don't you come back tomorrow, Vince, and we'll *really* talk."

He came back the following afternoon and she had a few members of the gang in for drinks and guitar playing. She got down some bourbon and danced a few steps. Finally the entourage drifted away. She sank into a chair and said exhaustedly, "What the hell do you want to do this for?" They both roared with laughter simultaneously, remembering their first meeting 13 years earlier, and the similar discussion of the script of *Lone Star*. "A high-class kept woman!" she shouted. Then she looked depressed. "Oh shit! You know I've been playing them all my life! People have come to think I'm a prostitute anyway! Type casting, they'll say! Oh well, I could walk through it, I guess." Sherman asked her to think it over. It was very late afternoon, and a tall, dark and handsome escort had arrived. It was time to leave.

Next night, Sherman went back to her suite for dinner. She was mellow, with several drinks under her belt, and they settled down happily to a meal prepared by her cook. "I'll confess something, Vince," she said finally. "I'm broke, and I desperately need the money. Someone crossed me up in the States and I have huge debts to people there. I don't want to do it but if you really want me, I'll try." They talked on, about Henry Miller, whom she had just met, about paintings, books, and music until the small hours. But finally negotiations for her to make the picture fell through.

Late in 1965, Ava was back in the news when she ducked cameramen during a visit to Basin Street East and an unidentified escort lunged at a cameraman, shouting, "You can get your head broken for that." She fled from the nightclub and drove off into the night. In January of the following year, she was having a series of gynecological problems. She spent several days at the Chelsea Hospital for Women having a checkup.

In the mid-1960s Ava began telling friends she was tired of Spain, and in 1967 and 1968 she made arrangements to move to London permanently. She started saying that the endless late nights at *tablaos flamencos* had bored her for some time.

Gossips said she had been asked to leave by the Spanish government. But the real reason for her decision to leave Spain was taxation. She had been incapable of avoiding taxation because of her innate honesty. As a result, the Spanish government overcharged her outrageously on her earnings. She protested, saying that the Spanish government should give her a medal, but her pleas were useless and in early 1968 she moved finally from Spain.

In the summer of 1968, after taking a flat above Park Lane in London, Ava made a trip to the Virgin Islands, and instantly fell in love with them. She adored St. Thomas and St. Croix, with their sheets of blue water, white yacht sails, and plunging green hills, their small white beaches and lovely hotels. She even planned to settle in the region, hoping to find an old mansion or convent which she could convert into a retreat from the world. At last she seemed to have a degree of financial security: her business agent, the Morgan Maree company in Hollywood, had invested wisely for her for some years, and the time seemed to have come to retire.

Finally she settled on living in London. She withdrew more and more from the world as though, like Garbo before her, she did not want people to see her visibly aging. But the cruel unflattering photographs went on and on.

Late in 1967, Ava began work as the 60-year old Empress of Austria in a remake of *Mayerling*, the story of the tragic love affair of the Crown Prince of Austria and his teenage girlfriend Maria Vetsera, which culminated in their double suicide on January 30, 1889. Ava was scarcely excited by the script, but she enjoyed the company of James Mason, cast as her husband the Emperor Franz Joseph, and she patiently played her part at the Studios de Boulogne in Paris.

Mason recalls that her wit hadn't faded. When Jane Fonda, then notable for the parts she had played naked for her husband, Roger Vadim, appeared on the set, Ava told a maid, "Tell her to come right over here and take all her clothes off!"

The film was a pretentious bore, directed by Terence Young, who had made some of the James Bond pictures, and much of the $5 million it cost went down the drain. The reviews were lamentable and these may well have accelerated Ava's desire to leave the screen permanently.

While she was in Paris for studio interiors for *Mayerling*, staying at the superdeluxe L'Hotel, she was pursued relentlessly by the horror writer Guy Des Cars, who was determined to date her. He arranged for a table next to hers in various expensive restaurants, called her suite constantly, and begged her to appear in one of his horror films. Finally she agreed to speak to him on the telephone, saying, "I'm not ready for a horror picture yet. I'm just a miserable lonely woman who should never have been a film star. But I'm not a freak. Goodbye."

For more than a year, Ava did nothing except rest, travel, and occasionally give small and intimate parties at her flat. Among her visitors was Roddy McDowall, an earnest celebrity-obsessed former child actor. Together with George Cukor and Sidney Guilaroff, he had now become a member of her tiny, mutually protective circle of intimate friends, and he had little difficulty in persuading her to appear in a movie which he would direct: *Tam-Lin*, to be co-produced by Alan Ladd, Jr., and Stanley Mann.

The title was changed from *Tam-Lin* to *Toys, Games*

and Toys, Tom Lynn, and several others before, under the title *Toys*, it began shooting for Commonwealth United in July 1969. It was the story of an immensely rich widow, Michaela Cazaret, played by Ava, who sustains a group of young people, mostly worthless hangers-on, who keep her entertained and interested in life. When she loses her lover to a cleric's daughter she works out a complicated revenge.

The film was shot at Pinewood Studios near London and in an ancient country mansion in Scotland. Sidney Guilaroff flew in to London and stayed at the Dorchester to dress Ava's hair. She went to Paris to be fitted for an expensive Balmain wardrobe. She had to learn lines like, "Life is an illusion. Therefore nothing is permanent."

A reporter from a magazine managed to pin her down for an interview. He said to her: "You are accused of destroying yourself. They say that you have lost all your friends, one by one. That you drown yourself in alcohol and orgies. That you like to slap people around, that you throw champagne—including the glass—at photographers."

Ava laughed: "Is that all? You haven't forgotten anything? I can go on. I have thrown 25 brand-new pairs of shoes into a well and a few ashtrays out of the window." Though later she was much kinder about her ex-husbands, on this occasion she was savage: "Mickey Rooney was only five feet tall, but above all he was young and vain. Artie Shaw was only a clarinetist, but he gave himself the airs of a cultured man without having any real culture. He learned a few pages of Dostoevski by heart and recited them at breakfast. Frank Sinatra was a sacred monster. He was convinced there was nobody in the world except him."

The circumstances of my meeting with Roddy McDowall were, to say the least, peculiar. We sat in his caravan at 20th Century-Fox. Sipping Seven-Up through a straw, he presented an extraordinary sight: he was wearing monkey makeup for his starring role in *Escape from the Planet of the Apes*. The makeup, which presented me with not one but two formidable rows of teeth, and twinkling shrewd eyes which may or may not have been his own, seemed weirdly at odds with his cool, level voice, the voice of a man who has worshipped at the feet of stars. He said: "The film broke my heart. I felt I never wanted to direct again. It was ruined by interference from the studio, which kept changing things around when I delivered the cuts. I think they were afraid of it, it was too strange and too original. Ava was wonderful in it. She had a fantastic strange aloof quality that was perfect for Michaela Cazaret. She instinctively understood the woman's innate fantastic wickedness and her sheer style."

Later, Ava told friends she hated *Tam-Lin* but would have done almost anything for Roddy, whom she adored.

The film turned out to be a thoroughly ridiculous example of camp Gothic, with Ava dressed up like Madam Gin Sling in *The Shanghai Gesture*. After shooting finished in December 1969, Commonwealth United collapsed, and the film was recut and released as *The Devil's Widow* in barely recognizable form. It disappeared at once.

After this catastrophe and that of *Mayerling*, it took someone as strong as John Huston to force Ava Gardner into working further in movies. He persuaded her to play the cameo role of Lily Langtry in *The Life of the Late Judge Roy Bean*, written by John Milius.

This was the story of a 19th century reformed bank robber turned hanging judge who cleans up a whole town in Arizona by killing off most of the inhabitants, and then renames it Langtry as a tribute to Lily Langtry, a theatrical star of his day with whom he is obsessed.

Ava was to appear briefly in the last scene, visiting a

Ava trying her hand at bullfighting from horseback at the private ranch
of Angel Peralta; she suffered her accident in this bullring
(UNITED PRESS INTERNATIONAL PHOTO)

Opposite: In the costume of the Duchess of Alba
for *The Naked Maja* (WIDE WORLD PHOTOS)

Left: With Fred Astaire between scenes of *On the Beach*. *Below*: Seated with Gregory Peck during filming of *On the Beach* (UNITED PRESS INTERNATIONAL PHOTO)

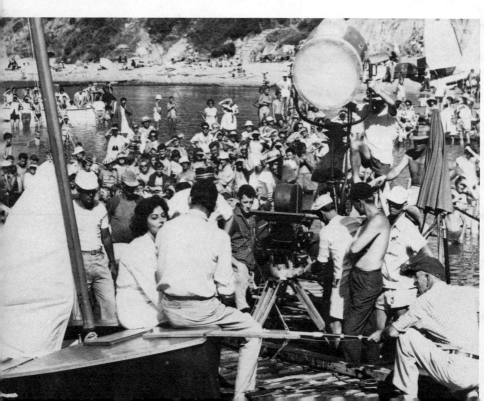

Above: With Dirk Bogarde
in *The Angel Wore Red*
(M-G-M). *Right*: With
Charlton Heston in *Fifty-five
Days at Peking*

With Kirk Douglas in *Seven Days in May*
(JOEL PRODUCTIONS, INC.)

Above: With Richard Burton, Cyril Delevanti, and Deborah Kerr
in *Night of the Iguana* (M-G-M). *Below*: With Richard Burton
in a scene from *Night of the Iguana* (M-G-M)

Left: Ava as Sarah, wife of Abraham, in *The Bible* (20TH CENTURY-FOX). *Below*: John Huston instructs Ava for a close-up scene in *The Bible* (WIDE WORLD PHOTOS)

With Omar Sharif in *Mayerling* (M-G-M)

small museum which had been built in honor of the Judge.

Richard Moore, the cameraman on the picture, says: "We were very doubtful whether Ava would show up for the shooting at all. I also was made to feel a degree of pressure: I had photographed Mae West in *Myra Breck-inridge* and I was afraid I'd have to do the same 'cosmetic job' on Ava. I needn't have worried.

"She arrived for three days' work, and the producer John Foreman, his secretary, Huston and his then fiancée (they've since married) CeeCee, Huston's secretary, and a couple of others got together for a welcome dinner for Ava that first night. She looked sensational, very graceful and completely at ease. I was nervous, and got stoned, but I noticed she was off the bottle.

"Next morning early—that's how rushed this was—she simply ruffled through some dresses the designer Edith Head had brought for her—she picked out an orchid dress and matching hat. Bill Tuttle, the dean of makeup artists, came to take care of her, and she told him and me that she didn't want to look unnaturally old. I suggested we use 'moondust,' powdered mica, to be sprinkled around the eyes to give an effect of aging, but she rejected that—so we settled on a very simple makeup. We'd been using a light fog filter for the whole picture, so we could easily give her the 'diffused look' used for stars of her age. She walked through the scenes beautifully, then asked to see the dailies. I was terrified they would be spoiled—I remember Mae West's were a reddish color in *Myra Breckinridge*, which I shot, and she was *mad*. But thank God that unpredictable Eastman stock worked out okay. She liked herself in the shots, she wasn't effusive, but she nodded her approval. Third day, the instant her job was

As Lily Langtry in *The Life of the Late Judge Roy Bean*
(UNITED PRESS INTERNATIONAL PHOTO)

done, she left. I can't blame her. Tucson was one hell of a hole in the wall for a star to be in."

While they were on location in Tucson, in November 1971, Ava discovered that George C. Scott was shooting *Rage* nearby, and, much to John Huston's fury, despite everything became friendly with him. According to Earl Wilson, Huston forbade Scott to come on the set, but Ava told Wilson, "George and I kept ducking under the guards."

She told a writer for *Ladies' Home Journal*: "I was glad to have the part because they paid $50,000. I was planning to go waterskiing in Acapulco anyway and it more than paid for the trip. So what the heck?"

In New York and London in the early 1970s, Ava resumed her friendship with Frank Sinatra. She was infuriated when his daughter Nancy wrote to her saying she was writing a biography of her father and wanted "anecdotes by those close to him." "Close to him?" Ava fumed. "Doesn't she know I was married to him?"

Despite her own widely quoted sharp remarks, she became violent when anyone criticized her previous husbands. In 1972, she gave a party for Artie Shaw. When one of the guests said that if Mickey Rooney were present his head would barely be seen over her coffee table, she shouted, "He's a giant compared with you!" She was furious with Rex Reed, who in a cruelly frank *Esquire* interview with her showed her dismissing her marriage to Mickey with the words, "Love Came to Andy Hardy," and who showed her getting drunk, swearing at everyone, and behaving outrageously.

In the early 1970s, Ava withdrew almost completely from the public eye. She still dismissed her films out of hand. Rex Reed reported that she sneered when he mentioned *Mogambo* as one of her good films. When *Red-*

book asked her if she hadn't at least liked *Night of the Iguana*, she said: "I certainly had high hopes for [it], first because I love and trust John [Huston]; second, because I was determined to do my best in the film. I even made myself look awful. I had lines penciled in under my eyes, because it was that kind of part. And what happened? When the film came out, instead of giving me credit for trying, the critics just said: 'Ava has lost her looks.'"

The statement simply isn't true; no critic of any major paper made any such remark. Her belief that this was said shows that after 30 years of stardom Ava still has a deep inferiority complex. But it is an inferiority complex tempered by a still graceful self-mocking humor. A widely reported story told by herself had her running into Bette Davis in the lobby of a Madrid hotel. "Miss Davis," she said, "I have admired you all my life. I'm Ava Gardner and I'm a great fan of yours." "Of course you are, my dear," Bette Davis replied. "Of course you are."

The one thing Ava still could not bear was to sleep alone. This is not to say that she has had numerous affairs in the 1970s. "Ava today is chaste," John Huston says. "She's become tired of passion. In a sense she always was. She only loved one man at a time, she was never promiscuous. Three husbands and maybe six lovers —that's a remarkable record for a woman of her beauty and fame and attraction."

But she cannot be alone at night. Someone, platonically, must be with her in the same room, often with the door open. A secretary who worked for her told producer Jack Sher: "I remember we suddenly went to Mexico for no reason. We got to a hotel room and she asked me to come in. I was terrified. I had heard rumors of lesbianism. I lay down on the bed in a nightgown wondering if I should open a window, scream, and run. Suddenly I felt her touch me. I *wanted* to scream. But all she did was hold my hand. Like a child. Afraid. She clung to me all night, and there wasn't a hint of sexuality."

In 1972, Ava was living in a five-story house in Alexander Square. *Ladies' Home Journal* writer Rowena Caldwell reported: "Ava Gardner sleeps alone in a narrow, four-poster bed on the second floor . . . there are steel grills on every window and two locks on all outside doors. One door in the basement had three locks; it leads to the wine cellar. . . . The four poster, made of brass and sheathed in delicate white lace, comes from the Flea Market in Madrid . . . it is three feet wide, not even spacious enough to be what London bed salesmen refer to discreetly as "an occasional two." In it, most midnights, Ava lies reading, munching Maltesers—an English malt-flavored candy—and wishing she had someone to cuddle."

Later, she took an apartment in Ennismore Gardens, Kensington, in a converted Victorian house fitted with barred windows because of a local rash of burglaries. It is still furnished with some of the somber, elegant antiques which she bought in flea markets and auctions for her house, La Bruja, in Madrid. Her closest friend in London is the actor Charles Gray, who lives opposite her. She is still very close to Frank Sinatra, who helps her considerably financially, and who has grown far mellower and more considerate toward her with the passage of time. She keeps in touch with Mickey Rooney and Artie Shaw, and with old Hollywood friends like the Greg Pecks, Minna Wallis, Phyllis Kirk, Sue Carol (Mrs. Alan) Ladd, and Lucille Ball. Visitors from the old M-G-M days (especially Sidney Guilaroff) are always welcome in London. She loves to drink at her local pub in Kensington, and to wander the streets with her corgi dog at night, talking to strange people. Her servants are often changed.

In February 1974, Ava returned to Hollywood to appear in the MCA-Universal epic *Earthquake*—in which she plays a woman jealous of her husband Charlton Heston's attentions to the younger Genevieve Bujold, yet trapped with both Heston and Bujold in a cellar while Los Angeles is destroyed by a cataclysm. As always on her Hollywood visits, she stayed quietly with Bappie in Bappie's quite modest home on Rinconia Drive, in the Hollywood Reservoir district. She dined out seldom, lunched once or twice at the English pub-like "Cock and Bull," attended only one major party (a charity affair for the black district of Watts) and occasional private parties given by Lew Wasserman, boss of MCA, or George Cukor. She was often seen walking her sister's dog in the remote Hollywood Hills, and she called her London home to hear her own dog barking, and even wrote him letters which were read to him in full. She went shopping with British reporter Roy Moseley in Beverly Hills, snapped at a headwaiter in the Brown Derby on Wilshire, flew off the handle at a new hairdresser, but generally behaved well. She cut out drinking (except for wine) for long periods of shooting, behaved with her director, Mark Robson (despite their miserable experience on *The Little Hut*), and graciously made up for old differences with Charlton Heston on *Fifty-five Days at Peking*.

Everyone who sees her says she has aged gracefully, drinks more sparingly, and has mellowed and grown sweeter with time. She still has her business interests in Hollywood, controlled by the investment company of Morgan Maree; they have handled her affairs for almost 30 years.

Although she is liable to insist that she is still a hillbilly and would in fact make a better secretary than she would an actress (she is still inordinately proud of her short-hand speed at the Atlantic Christian College), Ava is in fact today a well-read, well-informed woman, somewhat to the left in politics, hypersensitive about injustices, intensely liberal, and passionately interested in current events. Her indifference or contempt for her career as a whole is an actress's disguise for what in fact has been a total dedication to her art. She has always said, like Marlon Brando, that she only works for the money, but watch her on a set, exhausted by her own intense concentration, edgy, deeply absorbed, and you know her cool commercialism is a pose. The reason she so seldom performs is evidently the fear that she may wear out her resources. Her illness of the late 1960s, when she underwent major surgery, quite clearly frightened her. She hasn't forgotten her mother's early death from breast cancer.

Though Ava is not, and never will be, a great actress— a Garbo, a Hepburn, a Davis—she remains more sensitive and responsive than a Lana Turner, a Rita Hayworth, a Kim Novak. "Ava is on the level," George Cukor says. "She has a fundamental honesty, she puts her life into her playing." Her best acting has always been an extension of her wounded heart and soul; it is as though her eyes, despite the casual contemptuous laughter, were crying out for help. It is her vulnerability that makes her famous underplaying convincingly human. If she had had more technique and better luck she would have been a great actress, as well as a great star. As it is, she is a courageous mirror of her suffering on the screen, a fact which makes her more accessible to the sympathetic, quiets the envious, and awakens the man in men, the mother in women.

It is just because she has drunk hard, loved hard, sworn hard, gone sleepless, argued like a truck driver, "gone for the throat," that she seems the most accessible and likable of the great stars. She has been called a "mere" beauty, but compare her to Raquel Welch or Ann-Margret and the difference is obvious at once. Hollywood's history is peopled with tough, implacable beauties. Hurt and tender women are more common to French and Italian films. With worse looks and more temperament and talent, she might have been a Magnani, and she may yet emerge as one of those wonderful ravaged European stars, tearing passions to fine tatters.

It is clear that she faces life today with more equanimity, far more intelligent consideration, than she did 20 years ago. The agony of her life seems, at last, to have ebbed away, leaving her a look of poised, aloof serenity. In London, living her life of calm withdrawal, she has achieved a measure of peace. In her apartment behind barred windows in Kensington, she has at last found her island.

Of course, there are still the ironies. According to report, Howard Hughes sent her 50 red roses on her fiftieth birthday, December 24, 1972 ("The son-of-a-bitch," Nunnally Johnson commented. "Why couldn't he have sent her 30?"). Her friendship with Hughes resumed in London when he fled there after his hotel was stricken by an earthquake in Nicaragua.

But on the whole, Ava today is free of the tensions of love. She is fundamentally alone, as perhaps she always wanted to be. It has been a long way from Tobacco Road to finding that out. One welcomes the fact of her peace. Doesn't everyone like a happy ending?

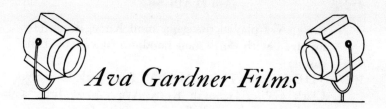

Ava Gardner Films

NOTE: Some of Ava Gardner's pictures were released out of the sequence in which she made them. Between 1942 and 1945, Ava appeared only in walk-ons and supporting or minor featured roles. The following is a list of the films (with release dates) in which she starred.

1945: WHISTLE STOP. United Artists. Dir., Léonide Moguy. George Raft. Ava played a girl in love with a ne'er-do-well in a small town.

1946: THE KILLERS. Universal. Dir., Robert Siodmak. Burt Lancaster, Edmond O'Brien, Albert Dekker. In this extension of Hemingway's famous short story, Ava played the gang moll Kitty, deceitfully involved with the young hoodlum played by Lancaster.

1947: THE HUCKSTERS. M-G-M. Dir., Jack Conway. Clark Gable, Deborah Kerr. Ava played Jean, a good-time girl who falls in love with Gable but is rejected in favor of prim-and-proper war widow Kerr.

SINGAPORE. Universal. Dir., John Brahm. Fred MacMurray, Roland Culver. Ava was a tragic war victim who has lost her memory in a bombing raid of Singapore. When special agent MacMurray returns postwar, she resumes her affair with him.

1948: ONE TOUCH OF VENUS. Universal. Dir., William A. Seiter. Robert Walker, Eve Arden, Tom Conway. In this version of the Kurt Weill musical, Ava played the Mary Martin role of a department store goddess brought to life by floorwalker Robert Walker's kiss.

THE GREAT SINNER. M-G-M. Dir., Robert Siodmak. Gregory Peck, Ethel Barrymore, Melvyn Douglas, Agnes Moorehead. Ava was Pauline, daughter of an inveterate card player, in this version of Dostoevski's novel *The Gambler*.

1949: EAST SIDE, WEST SIDE. M-G-M. Dir., Mervyn LeRoy. James Mason, Barbara Stanwyck. In this story of the New York upper crust, Ava was a sexy nightclub singer whom Mason dallies with while married to Stanwyck.

THE BRIBE. M-G-M. Dir., Robert Z. Leonard. Robert Taylor, Charles Laughton, John Hodiak. In this turkey, Ava was an unhappy girl married to cardiac case Hodiak but interested in counterespionage expert Taylor.

1950: MY FORBIDDEN PAST (also known as CAR-

RIAGE ENTRANCE). RKO. Dir., Robert Stevenson. Robert Mitchum, Melvyn Douglas. Set in New Orleans in the 19th century, this is the story of the fateful love of Ava for Robert Mitchum.

1951: PANDORA AND THE FLYING DUTCHMAN. M-G-M. Dir., Albert Lewin. James Mason, Mario Cabre, Harold Warrender. Ava was a 1931 playgirl in Spain who meets and becomes involved with mysterious yachtsman Mason. He turns out to be the Flying Dutchman.

SHOW BOAT. M-G-M. Dir., George Sidney. Howard Keel, Kathryn Grayson, Joe E. Brown, William Warfield. Ava played Julie, the tragic mulatto created by Helen Morgan on stage and in an earlier screen version.

1952: LONE STAR. M-G-M. Dir., Vincent Sherman. Clark Gable, Lionel Barrymore. Ava played a tempestuous Texas newspaperwoman in this story of Andrew Jackson and Texas' fight against the Union.

THE SNOWS OF KILIMANJARO. 20th Century-Fox. Dir., Henry King. Gregory Peck, Susan Hayward, Hildegarde Neff. In this version of Hemingway's celebrated *Esquire* story, Ava was the lost Twenties girl who dies during the Spanish Civil War.

1953: RIDE, VAQUERO. M-G-M. Dir., John Farrow. Robert Taylor, Howard Keel. Ava was married to rancher Keel but menaced by bandit Taylor in this Western set in 19th century Utah.

MOGAMBO. M-G-M. Dir., John Ford. Clark Gable, Grace Kelly. Ava played Honey Bear, a chorus girl stranded in Africa, in this version of *Red Dust*.

1954: KNIGHTS OF THE ROUND TABLE. M-G-M. Dir., Richard Thorpe. Robert Taylor, Mel Ferrer.

This was an adaptation of the tales of King Arthur's knights, in which Ava was Guinevere to Taylor's Lancelot.

THE BAREFOOT CONTESSA. United Artists. Dir., Joseph L. Mankiewicz. Humphrey Bogart, Rossano Brazzi, Warren Stevens. Ava played a woman based on Rita Hayworth, a Spanish dancer who becomes involved with several men, including Bogart and Howard Hughes-like multimillionaire Stevens.

1956: BHOWANI JUNCTION. M-G-M. Dir., George Cukor. Stewart Granger, Bill Travers. Ava was Victoria, an unhappy Eurasian girl, in this version of John Masters' novel of postwar India.

1957: THE LITTLE HUT. M-G-M. Dir., Mark Robson. Stewart Granger, David Niven, Walter Chiari. Ava was a showgirl stranded on a tropical island with three handsome men.

THE SUN ALSO RISES. 20th Century-Fox. Dir., Henry King. Tyrone Power, Mel Ferrer, Robert Evans. Ava played Lady Brett, an unhappy woman in love with the impotent Tyrone Power, in this version of Hemingway's classic novel.

1959: THE NAKED MAJA. M-G-M. Dir., Henry Koster. Anthony Franciosa. Ava was a violent Duchess of Alba, patroness and lover of the painter Goya, played by Franciosa.

ON THE BEACH. United Artists. Dir., Stanley Kramer. Gregory Peck, Fred Astaire. In this story about the end of the world following an atomic holocaust, Ava played a sad Australian party girl in love with scientist Peck.

1960: THE ANGEL WORE RED. M-G-M. Dir., Nunnally Johnson. Dirk Bogarde. Ava was a prostitute in love with priest Bogarde during the Spanish Civil War.

1963: FIFTY-FIVE DAYS AT PEKING. Allied Artists. Dir., Nicholas Ray. Charlton Heston, David Niven. Ava was the wife of Niven in this story of the Boxer Rebellion in China.

1964: SEVEN DAYS IN MAY. Paramount. Dir., John Frankenheimer. Burt Lancaster, Edmond O'Brien. Ava played a Washington society hostess whose help is sought in disrupting a fascist anti-Presidential plot.

NIGHT OF THE IGUANA. M-G-M. Dir., John Huston. Richard Burton, Deborah Kerr, Sue Lyon. Adapted from Tennessee Williams' play, this had Ava as Maxine, a hotel-keeper in Mexico in love with the down-and-out Burton.

1966: THE BIBLE. 20th Century-Fox. Dir., John Huston. George C. Scott, Peter O'Toole. Ava was Sarah, the barren wife to Scott's Abraham, who allows him to father a child by another.

1968: MAYERLING. M-G-M. Dir., Terence Young. James Mason, Omar Sharif, Catherine Deneuve. Ava played the Empress Elizabeth of Austria in this version of the French film classic of the 1930s.

1970: THE DEVIL'S WIDOW (also known as TAM-LIN). Commonwealth United. Dir., Roddy Mc-Dowall. Ian McShane. Ava was a fabulously wealthy and evil leader of a bizarre clan.

1971: THE LIFE OF THE LATE JUDGE ROY BEAN. United Artists. Dir., John Huston. Paul Newman. Ava played Lily Langtry, whom grizzled Judge Roy Bean had been devoted to for years.

1974: EARTHQUAKE. Universal. Dir., Mark Robson. Charlton Heston, Genevieve Bujold, George Kennedy. Ava, as the jealous wife of Heston, detests his mistress, Genevieve Bujold, but is trapped with both of them in a cellar during a giant Los Angeles earthquake.

Index

C

Viertel, Salka, 179
Vogeler, Gertrude, 14

W

Wakeman, Frederick, 67
Wald, Jerry, 74
Wald, Jerry (producer), 210
Walker, Robert, 41, 74, 252
Wallers, Betty, 144, 208–209
Wallis, Hal B., 61, 66
Wallis, Minna, 39, 66, 246
Wanger, Walter, 61
Warfield, William, 253
Warren, Annette, 101
Warrender, Harold, *119*, 253
Wasserman, Lew, 247
Waterbury, Ruth, 9, 14–15, 22, 124, 168, 190, 196
We Were Dancing, 37
Weinstein, Harry, 228
Weiss, Milton, 13–15, 21
Welch, Raquel, 249
Welles, Orson, 54, 162
West, Mae, 243
Wheeler, Lyle, 115
When Ladies Meet, 15
Whistle Stop, 51–56, 61–62, *80*; credits, 251

Whitelaw, Sandy, 218
Wilding, Michael, 219
Williams, Harris, 159, 161, 208
Williams, Tennessee, 216, 217, 224
Wilson, Earl, 129, 244
Winsor, Kathleen, 58
Winters, Shelley, 186, 187
Withers, Googie, 192
Wynn, Keenan, 89

Y

Yank at Eton, A, 36
Yordan, Philip, 51–55, 210, 212
Young, Robert, 15, 43
Young, Terence, 231, 255
Yule, Joe, Jr. *See* Rooney, Mickey
Yule, Joe, Sr., 27

Z

Zanuck, Darryl, 114–115, 178, 180–181, 188–189
Zimbalist, Sam, 131